PARAGRAPH POWER

50 Engaging Mini-Lessons, Activities, and Student Checklists for Teaching Paragraphing Skills

Adele Fiderer

D1716749

SCHOLASTIC
PROFESSIONAL BOOKS

NEW YORK • TORONTO • LONDON • AUCKLAND • SYDNEY
MEXICO CITY • NEW DELHI • HONG KONG • BUENOS AIRES

Acknowledgments

I would like to thank the following people who have made this book possible: Scholastic executive editor, Wendy Murray, who suggested the topic; my manuscript editor, Ray Coutu, whose excellent advice helped me improve the text; and my husband, Martin, who barbecued our dinner when I was deep into the endless composing and rewriting process. I am also grateful to all of my students over the years whose writings fill this book.

—Adele Fiderer

Front cover design by Hamid Rahmanian
Interior design by Solutions by Design, Inc.
Front cover photograph by Vicky Kasala

ISBN 0-439-20577-8

ting a Two-Paragraph Book Report: Focus on Craft ¶ Paragraph Transitions ¶ Writing Three-Paragraph Piec
the Article's Paragraphs ¶ Opening and Closing Paragraphs ¶ Following
at's the Purpose of Each Paragraph? ¶ Dialogue Rules ¶ Untangle the Dialogue ¶ Who's Saying What? ¶ Speaking o
Assignments ¶ Teaching Paragraph Basics ¶ Exploring the Purpose of Paragraphs ¶ What Makes a Paragraph
a Paragraph with Strong Details ¶ Writing Two-Paragraph Pieces ¶ Studying the Structure of a Two-Parag

Contents

Introduction 6

....
PART ONE
....

TEACHING PARAGRAPH BASICS

MINI-LESSON 1: Exploring the Purpose of Paragraphs 10

STUDENT ACTIVITY: What Makes a Paragraph? 11

MINI-LESSON 2: Identifying the Parts of a Paragraph 13

STUDENT ACTIVITY: Take Apart the Paragraph 14

STUDENT ACTIVITY: Body Sentence or Closing Sentence? 15

MINI-LESSON 3: Investigating Different Types of Paragraphs 16

STUDENT ACTIVITY: What's My Type? 18

MINI-LESSON 4: Enhancing a Paragraph With Strong Details 19

STUDENT ACTIVITY: Dress It Up With Details 20

STUDENT ACTIVITY: Game Rules Rule! 21

Fun and Fast One-Paragraph Writing Assignments 22

OUTLINE GUIDE 1: Outline a Paragraph 23

SELF-ASSESSMENT CHECKLIST 1: Paragraph Editing Checklist 24

....
PART TWO
....

WRITING TWO-PARAGRAPH PIECES

MINI-LESSON 5: Studying the Structure of a Two-Paragraph Piece 26

STUDENT ACTIVITY: Dissect a Book Description 27

STUDENT ACTIVITY: Edit a Two-Paragraph Book Report 28

MINI-LESSON 6: Writing a Two-Paragraph Letter: Focus on Conventions 30

OUTLINE GUIDE 2: Outline a Two-Paragraph Letter 31

MINI-LESSON 7: Writing a Two-Paragraph How-To Piece: Focus on Details 33

STUDENT ACTIVITY: Break the Paragraph, Dig for Details 35

OUTLINE GUIDE 3: Outline a Two-Paragraph How-To Piece 37

MINI-LESSON 8: Writing a Two-Paragraph Book Report: Focus on Craft 38

STUDENT ACTIVITY: Get Crafty With a Two-Paragraph Report 39

STUDENT ACTIVITY: Break the Paragraph, Dig for Details, Part 2 43

OUTLINE GUIDE 4: Outline a Two-Paragraph Book Report 45

SELF-ASSESSMENT CHECKLIST 2: Writing Process Checklist 46

Prime Time to Teach: Paragraph Transitions

MINI-LESSON 9: Writing Transitions 48

STUDENT ACTIVITY: Track the Report's Transitions 50

STUDENT ACTIVITY: Look to Books for Transitions 52

PART THREE

WRITING THREE-PARAGRAPH PIECES

MINI-LESSON 10: Analyzing Three-Paragraph Reports 56

STUDENT ACTIVITY: Edit a Science Report 57

STUDENT ACTIVITY: Edit a History Report 59

STUDENT ACTIVITY: Edit a Book Report 61

STUDENT ACTIVITY: Write a Three-Paragraph Book Blurb 63

MINI-LESSON 11: Writing an Outline for a Three-Paragraph Report 64

STUDENT ACTIVITY: Match the Main Idea to the Paragraph 66

OUTLINE GUIDE 5: Outline a Three-Paragraph Report 67

MINI-LESSON 12: Analyzing a Three-Paragraph Article and Essay 69

STUDENT ACTIVITY: Find the Article's Paragraphs 70

STUDENT ACTIVITY: Find the Essay's Main Ideas 72

OUTLINE GUIDE 6: Outline a Three-Paragraph Article 73

OUTLINE GUIDE 7: Outline a Three-Paragraph Essay 75

Fun and Fast Three-Paragraph Writing Assignments 77

SELF-ASSESSMENT CHECKLIST 3: General Editing Checklist 79

Prime Time to Teach: Opening and Closing Paragraphs

MINI-LESSON 13: Looking at Powerful Opening and Closing Sentences 82

STUDENT ACTIVITY: Compare the "Before" and "After" Paragraphs 83

MINI-LESSON 14: Following Techniques Student Writers Use 85

STUDENT ACTIVITY: Name that Technique 86

MINI-LESSON 15: Analyzing Effective Opening and Closing Paragraphs 88

STUDENT ACTIVITY: Name that Technique, Part 2 90

PART FOUR

WRITING MULTI-PARAGRAPH REPORTS AND ESSAYS

MINI-LESSON 16: Using Book Blurbs to Improve Multi-Paragraph Writing 94

STUDENT ACTIVITY: What's Each Paragraph's Purpose? 95

STUDENT ACTIVITY: Report on the Reports' Paragraphs 96

STUDENT ACTIVITY: What's the Main Idea? 100

STUDENT ACTIVITY: What's the Main Idea?, Part 2 102

SELF-ASSESSMENT CHECKLIST 4: Report and Essay Editing Checklist 107

Prime Time to Teach: Dialogue Rules

MINI-LESSON 17: Paragraphing Dialogue 110

STUDENT ACTIVITY: Untangle the Dialogue 111

MINI-LESSON 18: Discovering Dialogue Rules in Literature 113

STUDENT ACTIVITY: Who's Saying What? 115

STUDENT ACTIVITY: Speaking of Paragraphs 117

Fun and Fast Dialogue-Writing Assignments 119

Rubrics to Assess Paragraphing and Writing Skills 122

Bibliography 128

THE ARTICLE'S PARAGRAPHS ¶ OPENING AND CLOSING PARAGRAPHS ¶ FOLLOWING TECHNIQUES STUDENT WRITERS USE ¶ WRITIN
T'S THE PURPOSE OF EACH PARAGRAPH? ¶ DIALOGUE RULES ¶ UNTANGLE THE DIALOGUE ¶ WHO'S SAYING WHAT? ¶ SPEAKING OF
TING ASSIGNMENTS ¶ TEACHING PARAGRAPH BASICS ¶ EXPLORING THE PURPOSE OF PARAGRAPHS ¶ WHAT MAKES A PARAGRAPH A

Introduction

If you've ever tried to wade through the essay of a student who hasn't been taught how to craft a multi-paragraph piece, you know how daunting it can be to think about helping that student. One of the best ways to put a student on the road to good writing is by starting with the paragraph and working toward longer pieces.

For that reason I always give my students this assignment, early in the school year: "Write a one-paragraph letter to me about a book you're reading now or one that you've recently read. Describe the main character's problem and tell me what you think of the book so far."

From the writing I receive, I learn so much about my students' reading preferences and their ability to articulate their feelings about literature. I also learn a lot about their ability to craft paragraphs. Take Jillian's letter, for example:

> Dear Dr. Fiderer,
>
> I am reading <u>Anastasia Ask Your Analyst</u> where Anastasia has a big problom. she relizes its not her parents and Sam (her little brother) who aren't normal, it's that she isn't normal. I am at the part where her and her mom are having a fight (she just asked her parents if she could go to an analyst). I also read <u>Anastasia Krupnick</u> and so far I like this one better. I'll tell you what happens next week. I'm glad I choze this book.
>
> Jillian

As I read, I notice that Jillian demonstrates basic skills of paragraph writing:

- ☀ In the opening, she introduces the main character's problem.

- ☀ In the body of the piece, she provides some details about the how the character tries to solve her problem.

- ☀ In the closing, she compares this book to another in the Anastasia series.

- ☀ Throughout, she follows some conventions such as indenting the first line and using punctuation.

By the end of the year, I want Jillian to continue doing these things and much more. Specifically, I want her to know that:

- ☀ A paragraph gathers together sentences with related ideas about the paragraph's topic.

- ☀ A typical paragraph includes one or two topic sentences, a body, and a closing sentence or sentences.

- ☀ In a multi-paragraph piece, such as an essay, report, or narrative, each paragraph has its own main idea, which is closely related to the topic of the whole piece.

- ☀ The opening sentence or sentences introduce the paragraph's topic.

- ☀ The sentences in the body of the paragraph provide details and examples that give the reader a clear impression of the writer's ideas.

- ☀ The closing sentence of a body paragraph leads the reader to the main idea of the next paragraph.

- ☀ The final paragraph of a multi-paragraph piece brings the piece to a close.

I'm sure these are the concepts you want your students to know, as well. That's why I wrote this book.

What This Book Contains

Each part begins with at least one mini-lesson designed to help you teach some aspect of paragraph writing—from basic conventions to issues of style. Your students will learn how to brainstorm, draft, and revise single and multi-paragraph pieces such as essays, reports, narratives, letters, instructions, and reviews.

After each mini-lesson there are reproducible activities to provide students with the practice they'll need to master the strategy on their own. These activities make great homework assignments and assessment tools, too. They are designed to be fun and effective. Within parts, you will find reproducible Outline Guides and Checklists to help your students plan and assess their writing.

In the "Prime Time to Teach…" sections, you'll find lessons and activities on topics to help turn good pieces into great ones: writing transitions, opening and closing paragraphs, and dialogue.

I wish you much success as you experiment with the materials in this book. Look in the table of contents for a lesson that meets your students' needs, and you'll be on your way.

Adele Fiderer

PART ONE

TEACHING PARAGRAPH BASICS

NG A TWO-PARAGRAPH BOOK REPORT: FOCUS ON CRAFT ¶ PARAGRAPH TRANSITIONS ¶ WRITING THREE-PARAGRAPH PIECES ¶ WR THE ARTICLE'S PARAGRAPHS ¶ OPENING AND CLOSING PARAGRAPHS ¶ FOLLOWING TECHNIQUES STUDENT WRITERS USE ¶ WRITING 'S THE PURPOSE OF EACH PARAGRAPH? ¶ DIALOGUE RULES ¶ UNTANGLE THE DIALOGUE ¶ WHO'S SAYING WHAT? ¶ SPEAKING OF NG ASSIGNMENTS ¶ TEACHING PARAGRAPH BASICS ¶ EXPLORING THE PURPOSE OF PARAGRAPHS ¶ WHAT MAKES A PARAGRAPH A P

MINI-LESSON 1

Exploring the Purpose of Paragraphs

INTRODUCTION: It's always a good idea to find out what students already know about a new subject before you introduce it. So to find out what your students know about paragraphs, write these questions on the chalkboard: "What is a paragraph?" and "Why do we use paragraphs in our writing?" Have students write their responses or call them out while you record them on the chalkboard.

This lesson will help students understand how paragraphs help readers navigate text. It will introduce them to the main parts of a paragraph and their purposes.

MATERIALS

☀ For grade 3: individual copies of Student Activity 1A (page 11)

☀ For grades 4–6: individual copies of Student Activity 1B (page 12)

☀ A copy of a textbook or novel for each student, writing paper or notebooks, pencils

SUGGESTIONS FOR TEACHING THE LESSON

1 Begin the lesson by saying something like: "Open a book you are reading to a page containing paragraphs. Imagine what this page would be like without paragraphs. I don't think that I would want to read a book, or even a page, that had no paragraph breaks."

2 Ask students to take a few minutes to read the page and try to figure out what rules writers follow for beginning a new paragraph.

3 Call on students to share their ideas. Possible responses:

☀ To show a different topic or idea

☀ To separate spoken words from description

☀ To separate different speakers in a conversation

☀ To group sentences with similar ideas together

4 Give feedback. "You've discovered important rules for paragraphing that we all need to keep in mind when we write. Let's take a close look at a student's pargraph." Distribute copies of Activity 1, allowing about 10 to 15 minutes to complete it.

5 When students have finished, call on them to explain their decisions. To get them started, you might want to ask, "What's the job of a paragraph's topic sentence?" "Its closing sentence?" "What goes into its body?" and "Why are details and examples important?"

STUDENT ACTIVITY **1A**

What Makes a Paragraph?

DIRECTIONS: Read the third graders' paragraphs below. Then underline the topic sentences and closing sentences in each one, and put brackets around the body of the paragraph.

Example:

My special place is an old willow tree. [When I'm upset or when I just feel like sitting, that's where I go to relax. It's special there because I like the way the leaves droop down in my face. I watch the people walk by and it seems like everyone is in a hurry but me. I sit there and daydream all alone. Sometimes I fall asleep under the shade of the willow tree.] That's why my special place is under the big willow tree.

　　　　—Kaitlin, third grader

My special place is where an old playground used to be. I go sledding there. [There's a lot of trees there, but my favorite is the one that I can still swing on. The swing is made by a strong rope tied to a stick on my favorite tree. There's a big hill there with lots of rocks and I have some picnics there.] Those are the reasons why I like my special place.

　　　　—Joanna, third grader

My special place I like the most is the Slattery's house. [Chuck and Chris are the shining stars in high school basketball and they live right next to me. We watch TV at their house. I like it when their dog Regis plays dead. I also like when Chris and Chuck crack funny jokes.] Now you know why the Slattery's house is my special place.

　　　　—Kevin, third grader

What Makes a Paragraph?

DIRECTIONS: Read the students' paragraphs below. Then identify the paragraphs' topic sentences, body sentences, and closing sentences as follows:

a. Underline the topic sentence of each paragraph.

b. Underline the closing sentence.

c. Use brackets ([ ]) to frame the body sentences.

Example:

There are three things I look for in a book. [First, I like to read a novel about a girl who has real life problems with friends or parents. The second thing I look for is a city setting. I live in a big city and know the good and bad parts of living here. Last, I prefer a book by one of my favorite authors like Judy Blume or Mavis Jukes because they really know what 10-year-old girls are like.] Now, do you have a book for me?

People should treat other people's books carefully. [I want my books to come back to me the way they looked when they were given to them. Most people treat other people's books worse because the books aren't theirs. I don't want my books' spines broken, pages wrinkled, or cover ruined.] People should treat books delicately, especially if the books belong to someone else.

　　—Fifth grader

If you're ever asked to organize a party game for a younger friend or relative, here's an idea you can try. [Give each player a deflated balloon. The players all stand in line. When you say "Go!" the first person in line must blow up the balloon till it's bigger than a grapefruit. After a few minutes yell, "Let it go!" The player stops blowing and tosses the balloon in front of her, to see how far it will go. The person whose balloon goes the farthest is the winner.] Both boys and girls will like this game.

　　—Sixth grader

MINI-LESSON 2

Identifying the Parts of a Paragraph

INTRODUCTION: I've found that letter writing offers students many advantages, including helping them develop paragraphing skills. In this lesson, students look closely at a letter to familiarize themselves with a paragraph's three main parts: topic sentence(s), body sentences, and closing sentence(s).

MATERIALS

☀ Individual copies of Student Activity 2 (page 14)

☀ Individual copies of Student Activity 3 (page 15)

☀ Individual copies of Self-Assessment Checklist 1 (page 24)

·············· SUGGESTIONS FOR TEACHING THE LESSON ··············

1. Begin by distributing Activity 2 to students and saying something like: "Read the letter a student wrote to her teacher describing a character in a book she read."

2. Ask students to underline the paragraph's topic sentences and closing sentence, and use brackets to frame the body sentences of the paragraph. If they're having trouble, you can remind them of the purpose of each kind of sentence—that topic sentences let the reader in on the "big idea" in an interesting way, body sentences provide details about that idea, and closing sentences sum up the idea so the reader isn't left hanging.

3. Check students' work:

   <u>I am reading _Anastasia Ask Your Analyst._</u> That's a good title because Anastasia does have a big problem. [She realizes that it's not her parents and Sam, her little brother, who aren't normal—it's that she isn't normal. I am at the part where Anastasia and her mom are having a fight because she just asked her parents if she could go to an analyst.] <u>I'm glad I chose this book because I like to read books about girls my age and their problems.</u>

4. For additional practice in identifying body and closing sentences, distribute Activity 3. (Answers: 1. B   2. C   3. B   4. B)

5. Have students write one-paragraph letters to you describing a character in a story they have read recently or are currently reading.

6. Give each student a copy of Self-Assessment Checklist 1 to use before and after they write.

Take Apart the Paragraph

DIRECTIONS: Underline the topic sentences and closing sentence in the letter below, and use brackets ([ ]) to frame its body sentences.

January 3

Dear Mrs. Smith:

I am reading *Anastasia Ask Your Analyst.* [That's a good title because Anastasia does have a big problem. She realizes that it's not her parents and Sam, her little brother, who aren't normal—it's that she isn't normal. I am at the part where Anastasia and her mom are having a fight because she just asked her parents if she could go to an analyst.] I'm glad I chose this book because I like to read books about girls my age and their problems.

Sincerely,

Jillian

Paragraph Power ○ Scholastic Professional Books

Body Sentence or Closing Sentence?

DIRECTIONS: Read the following topic sentences of a paragraph:

> On January 30, six Edgewood classes went to Heathcote School. We witnessed a wonderful performance by David Novak that focused on trickster tales.

Now select body and closing sentences to add to these topic sentences. Write "B" for body sentence or "C" for closing sentence on the blank line after each sentence.

1. To prepare for the show, we went to a class once a week for about four weeks. In this class we experienced drama, expressing our feelings with oohs and ahhs. __B__

2. David Novak really got his message through. If there weren't so many tricksters, there wouldn't be so many fools. __C__

3. After hearing a story about a trickster, we then acted it out. __B__

4. David Novak shared many stories with us, such as Tom Sawyer, the Great Whitewasher, and The Fox and the Crow. And last but not least, he told an African folktale featuring that troublemaker, Anansi, the spider, and Anansi's wife. __B__

G A TWO-PARAGRAPH BOOK REPORT: FOCUS ON CRAFT ¶ PARAGRAPH TRANSITIONS ¶ WRITING THREE PARAGRAPH PIECES ¶ WRITING
HE ARTICLE'S PARAGRAPHS ¶ OPENING AND CLOSING PARAGRAPHS ¶ FOLLOWING TECHNIQUES STUDENT WRITERS USE ¶ WRITING
S THE PURPOSE OF EACH PARAGRAPH? ¶ DIALOGUE RULES ¶ UNTANGLE THE DIALOGUE ¶ WHO'S SAYING WHAT? ¶ SPEAKING OF P
G ASSIGNMENTS ¶ TEACHING PARAGRAPH BASICS ¶ EXPLORING THE PURPOSE OF PARAGRAPHS ¶ WHAT MAKES A PARAGRAPH A

MINI-LESSON

Investigating Different Types of Paragraphs

INTRODUCTION: As any writer knows, there are different types of paragraphs and each serves a specific purpose. A descriptive paragraph, for example, explains what something looks, sounds, and feels like. A narrative paragraph tells a story. An expository paragraph gives information. I've found that the following lesson works well for introducing those types of paragraphs to students.

MATERIALS

☀ Overhead transparency of the reproducible form "Types of Paragraphs" (page 17)

☀ Individual copies of Student Activity 4 (page 18)

.... SUGGESTIONS FOR TEACHING THE LESSON ....

1. To begin, tell students something like: "Today we are going to take a close look at three kinds of paragraphs, and discuss the different purposes each one serves. We'll also look at how writers build these paragraphs from different kinds of details."

2. Show the "Types of Paragraphs" transparency (page 17) and ask students to read the three example paragraphs. Be sure to cover the definition of each paragraph type.

3. When they have finished reading, ask, "So what do you think is the purpose of each kind of paragraph? What was the writer of each piece trying to do?" Possible responses:

    ☀ "Descriptive paragraphs tell you what a person, place, or thing looks like."

    ☀ "Narrative paragraphs are like stories. They tell you what happened first, second, third..."

    ☀ "Expository paragraphs use facts and details to explain things to you."

4. Reveal the transparency's definitions and compare them to students' responses.

5. Distribute Student Activity 4. Explain the assignment by saying something like: "Read the essay and decide whether each paragraph is descriptive, narrative, or expository. Sometimes it's difficult to make a decision. So you'll need to think about which term *best* describes most of the sentences in each paragraph. Use the 'Types of Paragraphs' form if you get stuck." Possible responses: paragraph 1: descriptive; 2: expository; 3: narrative; 4: narrative; 5: expository; 6: expository

6. Give students about 15 minutes to complete the assignment and discuss their responses.

TYPES OF PARAGRAPHS

Descriptive Paragraphs

A descriptive paragraph gives a clear picture of a person, place, object, event, or idea. Details for descriptive paragraphs come from the writer's senses—smell, taste, touch, hearing, and sight. These are known as sensory details.

Example:

Galdriel Hopkins (Gilly) is the main character in *The Great Gilly Hopkins* by Katherine Paterson. Gilly is a shabby-looking foster child who doesn't want to make herself pretty. Her hair is uncombed and usually has gum in it. She also makes weird noises with her gum while she is chewing it.

Narrative Paragraphs

A narrative paragraph gives the details of an experience or event in the order in which they happened.

Example:

Soon my new second-grade teacher came over to us and said a polite hello to my mother. "I am Mrs. Ames," my teacher said to my mother and me. I finished saying goodbye to my mother and I began to bite my nails as I shifted my weight from side to side, having absolutely no idea of what to do.

Expository Paragraphs

An expository paragraph gives directions or uses facts and details to explain information. The following paragraph is expository because it explains how to do an assignment.

Example:

Read the student's science report. On the blank line following each paragraph, write the letter *d* if the paragraph is descriptive, the letter *n* if the paragraph is narrative, or the letter *e* if the paragraph is expository. If a paragraph seems to combine types, select the one that best describes it.

STUDENT ACTIVITY **4**

What's My Type?

DIRECTIONS: Read the following essay. On the blank line after each paragraph, write the letter that describes the paragraph:

> D = Descriptive (Uses details to describe a person, place, object, event, or idea.)
>
> N = Narrative (Gives details of an event in the order they happened.)
>
> E = Expository (Uses facts to explain something.)

If a paragraph seems to combine types, select the one that best describes it.

Pond Life

I was at the pond enjoying the reddish brown water with little green leaves covering it and looking at little waves rolling in the pond when Liz suddenly shouted, "A bug, a bug!" **1.** _____

Just that second I screamed, "I caught a bug and it's big, too!" Dr. Frantz told me it was a damselfly and to call it a her. Her body looked like a small and thin leaf. **2.** _____

The next day in the science room, I dropped her into a little cup filled with water. Then I put the cup on a special microscope. It's special because it is made for bigger bugs that don't fit in normal microscopes. **3.** _____

At home I ran to my mother and asked her to bring me to the library to read about damselflies. I borrowed two books, *The Field Guide to North American Insects and Spiders* and *Observing Insect Lives*. When I read both books, I found out that Stacy was a Black Winged Damselfly. **4.** _____

These insects are called damselflies not because they are female, but because they look like females. They have brownish transparent wings, brown heads, yellow brown eyes, and dark brown bodies. They go very fast. They live along the edges of slow streams and ponds. When they are young they eat algae, but when they grow up they eat small insects. **5.** _____

The one I caught was a young damselfly, and also a naiad. Grown-up female damselflies lay eggs on soft plant stems beside the water. Eggs grow into naiads. Naiads grow into adults which fly out of the water. After learning about the damselfly I feel proud because I learned a lot. **6.** _____

Paragraph Power ○ Scholastic Professional Books

...ING A TWO-PARAGRAPH BOOK REPORT: FOCUS ON CRAFT ¶ PARAGRAPH TRANSITIONS ¶ WRITING THREE-PARAGRAPH PIECES ¶
ND THE ARTICLE'S PARAGRAPHS ¶ OPENING AND CLOSING PARAGRAPHS ¶ FOLLOWING TECHNIQUES STUDENT WRITERS USE ¶ WRIT
HAT'S THE PURPOSE OF EACH PARAGRAPH? ¶ DIALOGUE RULES ¶ UNTANGLE THE DIALOGUE ¶ WHO'S SAYING WHAT? ¶ SPEAKING
RITING ASSIGNMENTS ¶ TEACHING PARAGRAPH BASICS ¶ EXPLORING THE PURPOSE OF PARAGRAPHS ¶ WHAT MAKES A PARAGRAPH

MINI-LESSON 4

Enhancing a Paragraph With Strong Details

INTRODUCTION: Now that your students have an understanding of a paragraph's structure, they're ready to discover the essential element of a powerful paragraph: strong details. Whether they're writing a letter, a report, or a story, students must infuse their writing with details that are specific and sensory-rich to create pictures in their readers' minds. Here is how I help my students do that.

MATERIALS

☀ Individual copies of Student Activities 5 (page 20) and 6 (page 21)

·············· SUGGESTIONS FOR TEACHING THE LESSON ···············

1. On the chalkboard write, "As soon as I awoke this morning, I knew it was going to be a bad day, and it was." Then ask students, "When you read this opening line of a story, what do you think? What do you want to know? What questions does it raise? Turn to the classmate next to you and take a minute to share ideas."

2. Have students talk among themselves and then share their thoughts with the whole class. Guide them to see that the sentences that follow need to have details to give the reader a clear picture of a bad day. Invite students to offer sentences containing such details. For example, a student might suggest, 'I turned on the radio and heard the weather forecast—heavy rain all day.'"

3. Call on students to supply other details that show what makes a day bad. Encourage them to use their memories or imaginations to paint a word picture of a bad day.

4. If students are having problems getting started, give them a prompt such as, "When I opened the door to bring in the newspaper..." A student might say, "It was soaking wet" or "My dog ran away."

5. Continue to ask around the room until all students have had an opportunity to supply at least one detail about the bad day.

6. Distribute copies of Student Activity 5. Give students enough time to finish it and share responses as a class. For extra practice, hand out Activity 6.

Dress It Up With Details

DIRECTIONS: Look for a strong opening paragraph in a book you are reading or have recently read. Write it on the lines below.

_____

_____

_____

_____

_____

_____

_____

Choose one of these five topic sentences to create your own paragraph. On a separate sheet of paper, write out the sentence and finish the paragraph, adding details that will create vivid pictures in a reader's mind. Sum it up with a powerful closing sentence.

1. As soon as I awoke this morning, I knew it was going to be a bad day, and it was.

2. As soon as I awoke this morning, I knew it was going to be a great day, and it was.

3. As I walked to school carrying my homework folder, the sky grew dark. I heard a clap of thunder and then the sky opened up. It was the worst rainstorm ever.

4. "No TV for you this week," I imagined my dad saying as I handed him the note that my teacher had sent home with me. I knew what that note said, and I sure didn't want him to see it.

5. My parents warned me never to go near the deserted, broken-down house, but Jamie had talked me into going there with him. I knew it was going to be the scariest experience of my life.

Game Rules Rule!

DIRECTIONS: Read the following game-rules paragraph. Notice how the topic and closing sentences are underlined, and the body sentences are bracketed.

If you're ever asked to organize a party game for a younger friend or relative, here's an idea you can try. [Give each player a deflated balloon. The players all stand in line. When you say "Go!" the first person in line must blow up the balloon till it's bigger than a grapefruit. After a few minutes yell, "Let it go!" The player stops blowing and tosses the balloon in front of her, to see how far it will go.] The person whose balloon goes the farthest is the winner. Both boys and girls will like this game.

In one paragraph, write directions for playing a game you enjoy. Be sure to include vivid details in the topic, body, and closing sentences.

_____

_____

_____

_____

_____

_____

_____

_____

_____

_____

FUN AND FAST ONE-PARAGRAPH WRITING ASSIGNMENTS

We teachers are busy these days. There's so much to do and so little time. Here are some fun, effective, and fast assignments for writing single paragraphs. To ensure that students write a topic sentence, body sentences that expand on the topic, and a closing sentence, distribute the Outline Guide on page 23 to help them organize their thoughts. Also, distribute copies of the Paragraph Editing Checklist on page 24 and encourage students to make changes that will improve their writing.

IDEA 1: Write a one-paragraph ad to sell something real or ridiculous. For example, sneakers you've outgrown, last year's math book, your services as a babysitter or homework tutor, your old teddy bear, or a story you wrote.

IDEA 2: Write a one-paragraph letter to a mail-order company's complaint department, for one of these reasons.

- ☀ Your order has arrived one year late.

- ☀ You received the wrong item—a live tiger instead of a stuffed tiger.

- ☀ You received a healthy-recipes cookbook instead of the Harry Potter book you wanted.

- ☀ You are applying for a position as a customer service representative. Give the manager an example of what you would write to a dissatisfied customer.

IDEA 3: Write a one-paragraph review of your favorite or least-favorite television show. Or write a letter to the studio expressing your objection to too many commercials or your interest in being in the cast of a show.

Outline a Paragraph

DIRECTIONS: Use this form to help you organize and write a paragraph. It asks you to think about your paragraph's topic, body, and closing sentences.

What is the topic of your paragraph?

_____

Write your topic sentence or sentences, using examples you've seen as models.

_____

_____

_____

_____

What details do you want to cover in your paragraph? Make notes on them.

_____

_____

_____

_____

Write a closing sentence that sums up your topic and will leave your reader satisfied.

_____

_____

_____

_____

Name _____ Date _____

Paragraph Editing Checklist

DIRECTIONS: Listed below are key elements of a well-written paragraph. Review your writing and check off what you've done.

Paragraph Topic or Title _____

1 The first line of the paragraph is indented. . . . . □

2 The paragraph has one or two topic sentences that catch my
 reader's attention. . . . . □

3 The paragraph's body sentences have ideas, examples, and details
 that help explain my topic. . . . . □

4 The paragraph has one or two closing sentences that sum up my topic
 and will leave my reader satisfied. . . . . □

5 The paragraph contains

 correct spellings. . . . . □

 correct use of punctuation marks. . . . . □

 correct use of capital letters. . . . . □

6 Count up your check marks and rate your paragraph-writing skills:

 _____ 6 or 7 checks: Good

 _____ 4 or 5 checks: Improving

 _____ 3 checks or fewer: Needs Improvement

Paragraph Power ○ Scholastic Professional Books

PART TWO

WRITING TWO-PARAGRAPH PIECES

THE ARTICLE'S PARAGRAPHS ¶ OPENING AND CLOSING PARAGRAPHS ¶ FOLLOWING TECHNIQUES STUDENT WRITERS USE ¶ WRITIN
'S THE PURPOSE OF EACH PARAGRAPH? ¶ DIALOGUE RULES ¶ UNTANGLE THE DIALOGUE ¶ WHO'S SAYING WHAT? ¶ SPEAKING OF
NG ASSIGNMENTS ¶ TEACHING PARAGRAPH BASICS ¶ EXPLORING THE PURPOSE OF PARAGRAPHS ¶ WHAT MAKES A PARAGRAPH A
NCING A PARAGRAPH WITH STRONG DETAILS ¶ WRITING TWO-PARAGRAPH PIECES ¶ STUDYING THE STRUCTURE OF A TWO-PARAGR

MINI-LESSON

Studying the Structure of a Two-Paragraph Piece

INTRODUCTION: One of the most useful tools for teaching paragraph writing was on my classroom shelves for years before I realized it: the back-cover summaries of books. Now I always share summaries with students to teach them how two-paragraph pieces are structured.

MATERIALS

☀ Individual copies of Student Activities 7 (page 27) and 8 (page 28)

☀ Good examples of two-paragraph summaries from the backs of books

☀ A pile of a dozen or so paperback books students might read

················ SUGGESTIONS FOR TEACHING THE LESSON ···············

1 Introduce the lesson by pointing to the pile of books and asking students to think about how they might select one to read. "How do you decide?" Possible responses: "If it's by an author I like…" "If I've heard someone talk about it…" "If it's not too long…" and "I look at the back cover and read what it's about…"

2 Give feedback. Say something like: "You've mentioned several good reasons for selecting a particular book. I always look to see who the author is, too. Usually, I'll turn to the back cover to get an idea of what the story is about. These back-cover summaries tell me enough about the main character and plot to help me make my decision."

3 Read aloud a couple of good examples of two-paragraph summaries from the books in your pile.

4 Distribute copies of Activity 7. "Let's see what we can learn from the summary on the back cover of *Matilda* by Roald Dahl."

5 Ask students to identify the topic, body, and closing sentences of each paragraph, discussing why it's important for a paragraph to include each of these kinds of sentences. For extra practice, hand out Activity 8.

STUDENT ACTIVITY **7**

Dissect a Book Description

DIRECTIONS: Read the following two-paragraph description of characters in *Matilda*.

Matilda is a genius. Unfortunately her family treats her like a dolt. Her crooked car salesman father and loud, bingo-obsessed mother think Matilda's only talent is as a scapegoat for everything that goes wrong in their miserable lives. But it's not too long before the sweet and sensitive child decides to fight back. Faced with practical jokes of sheer brilliance, her parents don't stand a chance.

"The Trunchbull," however, is a different story. Miss Trunchbull, ex-Olympic hammer thrower and headmistress of Matilda's school, has terrorized generations of Crunchem Hall students—and teachers. But when she goes after sweet Miss Honey, the one teacher who believes in Matilda, she goes too far.

1 Topic sentences make the main idea clear. Copy the two topic sentences of paragraph one.

_____

_____

2 The body sentences of a paragraph provide details or examples that support the main idea. On the lines below, write the details in the body sentences that describe the way Matilda's family treats her.

_____

_____

3 The last two sentences sum up the main ideas in paragraph one. Copy them on the lines below.

_____

_____

4 In paragraph two, underline the opening and closing sentences, and put brackets ([ ]) around the body sentence.

STUDENT ACTIVITY **8A**

Edit a Two-Paragraph Book Report

DIRECTIONS: Each of the following book reports should be written as two paragraphs because they contain more than one main idea. Read the reports, find the sentences that introduce a new main idea, and place a paragraph mark (⌐) at the start of those sentences.

My Little Island

My Little Island is a great book about a boy and his friend Lucca as they visit a small Caribbean island. It has wonderful pictures of foods that make your mouth water—pawpaws, guavas, mangoes and many more. My favorite part is when the boys go to the forest and stand in the water and fish while listening to bird songs. This book made me feel like traveling around the world and it will probably do the same for you.

Julie of the Wolves

This book is about a 13-year-old girl named Miyax. She runs away from her husband to live the life of her Inuit Eskimo ancestors. She also travels through the Arctic to meet her pen pal in San Francisco who calls her Julie. On her way through the Arctic, she meets a pack of wolves. She learns how to communicate with them and they all become like brothers and sisters. I liked the book because it shows how the Inuit lived. It also shows how the Inuit are changing and it has a surprise ending!

Edit a Two-Paragraph Book Report
Check Your Work

DIRECTIONS: Compare your work to the writers'. Did you break the paragraphs in the same places?

My Little Island

My Little Island is a great book about a boy and his friend Lucca as they visit a small Caribbean island. It has wonderful pictures of foods that make your mouth water—pawpaws, guavas, mangoes and many more.

My favorite part is when the boys go to the forest and stand in the water and fish while listening to bird songs. This book made me feel like traveling around the world and it will probably do the same for you.

Julie of the Wolves

This book is about a 13-year-old girl named Miyax. She runs away from her husband to live the life of her Inuit Eskimo ancestors. She also travels through the Arctic to meet her pen pal in San Francisco who calls her Julie.

On her way through the Arctic, she meets a pack of wolves. She learns how to communicate with them and they all become like brothers and sisters. I liked the book because it shows how the Inuit lived. It also shows how the Inuit are changing and it has a surprise ending!

Reread the closing sentences of the four paragraphs above. Underline the one that you like best and explain why.

_____

_____

_____

_____

Student writings are from Scholastic's *Storyworks*, September 1995.

ING A TWO-PARAGRAPH BOOK REPORT: FOCUS ON CRAFT ¶ PARAGRAPH TRANSITIONS ¶ WRITING THREE-PARAGRAPH PIECES ¶ W
THE ARTICLE'S PARAGRAPHS ¶ OPENING AND CLOSING PARAGRAPHS ¶ FOLLOWING TECHNIQUES STUDENT WRITERS USE ¶ WRITIN
T'S THE PURPOSE OF EACH PARAGRAPH? ¶ DIALOGUE RULES ¶ UNTANGLE THE DIALOGUE ¶ WHO'S SAYING WHAT? ¶ SPEAKING OF
ING ASSIGNMENTS ¶ TEACHING PARAGRAPH BASICS ¶ EXPLORING THE PURPOSE OF PARAGRAPHS ¶ WHAT MAKES A PARAGRAPH A

MINI-LESSON

Writing a Two-Paragraph Letter: Focus on Conventions

INTRODUCTION: Writing a two-paragraph letter is a manageable task most students enjoy, particularly if they have a real reason for doing it. It's a great way to introduce paragraph-writing conventions.

To motivate your students, get *Free Stuff for Kids* (Meadowbrook Press) which features hundreds of no-cost or inexpensive products that kids can request in writing. I've also found that writing fan letters to favorite sports figures, TV stars, and authors is also appealing to students.

MATERIALS

- ☀ Individual copies and/or an overhead transparency of Outline Guide 2 (page 31)
- ☀ Lined paper for drafting and revising

SUGGESTIONS FOR TEACHING THE LESSON

1 Before class, on a chart or chalkboard, write the following topic ideas for letters, along with any other ideas you might have:

   - ☀ A fan letter to a favorite sports figure or musician
   - ☀ A letter to a relative thanking him or her for something
   - ☀ A letter to a friend who has moved away

2 Say something like: "How many of you like to receive letters in the mail? Have any of you written a letter to a family member or friend? Look at my list on the board. Can you think of other reasons for writing a letter?" Record students' ideas. Prompt them to brainstorm topics for letters of request, letters of protest, and letters to inform a group about an event. Then tell them, "Today you will write a two-paragraph letter to someone you know."

3 Read aloud a good example of a two-paragraph letter, perhaps from a children's book such as *Dear Mr. Henshaw* by Beverly Cleary.

4 Choose a sample topic and type of letter, show Outline Guide 2 on the overhead, and model how you outline a letter about that topic.

5 Write a draft of a letter on the overhead, using the outline guide as a reference.

6 Have students practice on a topic of their choice, using copies of Outline Guide 2.

Outline a
Two-Paragraph Letter

DIRECTIONS: Use this form to help you organize and write a two-paragraph letter.

Date: _____

Your address: _____

City, state, zip code: _____

Greeting: Dear _____ ,

Opening sentence: _____

_____

Main idea/details paragraph 1: _____

_____

_____

Main idea/details paragraph 2: _____

_____

_____

Closing sentence: _____

Closing remark: _____

Your name: _____

Strategies for Building Students' Paragraphing Skills Through Letter Writing

☀ Let students observe you compose a letter on large chart paper. As you write, point out the placement of the heading, greeting, body, and closing, as well as your use of paragraphs. Display this model so that students can refer to it when they write their own letters.

☀ Content-area studies, particularly those that involve students in relevant, real-life inquiries, offer students many opportunities to improve their paragraph-writing skills. For example, as part of an environmental study, you might ask students to write letters inviting experts to your classroom, or to write to the editor of your local newspaper about the importance of recycling.

☀ Read aloud letters to the editor from your local newspaper and ask students to write about a community issue that interests them.

☀ Invite students to correspond with sports figures. Players on local teams usually answer, often with an autographed photo. A listing of the mailing addresses of most living major-league baseball players can be obtained from the Jack Smalling Baseball Address List. Visit www.baseballaddresses.com for details.

☀ Getting free or inexpensive products is also good motivator. *Free Stuff for Kids* (Meadowbrook Press) features hundreds of things to write away for.

☀ In cooperation with another teacher in your school district or in a different state, pair up students for pen-pal correspondence.

☀ At the end of the school year, have your students write to students in the grade below, with tips on how to be successful in their next grade.

☀ For useful tips on teaching letter writing, see *Putting It in Writing* by Steve Otfinoski (Scholastic). *Sincerely Yours—How to Write Great Letters* by Elizabeth James and Carol Barkin (Houghton Mifflin) offers excellent advice to upper elementary students.

☀ Encourage students to use e-mail and other forms of Internet exchanges.

MINI-LESSON

Writing a Two-Paragraph How-To Piece: Focus on Details

INTRODUCTION: One of the best ways to help your students learn paragraphing customs, such as using vivid details to support main ideas, is to encourage them to "discover" those conventions for themselves in the books, newspapers, and magazines they read. This lesson, a favorite among my students, helps you reinforce the importance of supporting details by analyzing the work of one writer.

MATERIALS

☀ Individual copies and an overhead transparency of Student Activity 9 (page 35)

☀ Individual copies of Outline Guide 3: Two-Paragraph How-To Piece (page 37)

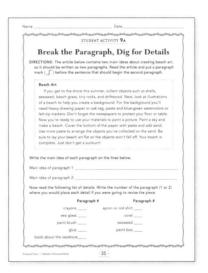

············· SUGGESTIONS FOR TEACHING THE LESSON ·············

1 Introduce the lesson by distributing Activity 9 and saying something like: "Your assignment today is to read the article 'Beach Art' to discover the paragraphing customs that writers follow."

2 Have students read the article all the way through to understand the writer's ideas. Then let them reread it for structure, looking for the point in the text where there should be a paragraph break. Have them use a paragraph mark (⌐) to show where the second paragraph should begin. (The most sensible place to break the article is at "Now you're ready to use your materials to paint a picture," since the writer is moving from preparation for the project to creation of the project.)

3 Compare answers and, as a class, talk about how and why we segment ideas into the paragraphs.

4 Have students determine the main idea of each paragraph and write their answers on the activity sheet.

5 Write the main ideas as headings on the board: "Preparing to Create Beach Art" and "Creating Beach Art." Ask students to sort the following details, which could be used in a revision of the piece, under the appropriate heading:

crayons	**apron or old shirt**
sea glass	**coral**
paint brush	**seaweed**
glue	**paint box**
book on the seashore	

6 Discuss responses as a class, using the overhead transparency of the activity as a reference.

7 Have students write their own two-paragraph how-to piece using Outline Guide 3 on page 37 to help them organize their thoughts.

STUDENT ACTIVITY **9A**

Break the Paragraph, Dig for Details

DIRECTIONS: The article below contains two main ideas about creating beach art, so it should be written as two paragraphs. Read the article and put a paragraph mark (⌐) before the sentence that should begin the second paragraph.

Beach Art

If you get to the shore this summer, collect objects such as shells, seaweed, beach grass, tiny rocks, and driftwood. Next, look at illustrations of a beach to help you create a background. For the background you'll need heavy drawing paper or oak tag, paste and blue-green watercolors or felt-tip markers. Don't forget the newspapers to protect your floor or table. Now you're ready to use your materials to paint a picture. Paint a sky and make a beach. Cover the bottom of the paper with paste and add sand. Use more paste to arrange the objects you've collected on the sand. Be sure to lay your beach art flat so the objects won't fall off. Your beach is complete. Just don't get a sunburn!

Write the main idea of each paragraph on the lines below.

Main idea of paragraph 1: _____

Main idea of paragraph 2: _____

Now read the following list of details. Write the number of the paragraph (1 or 2) where you would place each detail if you were going to revise the piece.

Paragraph #	**Paragraph #**
crayons _____	apron or old shirt _____
sea glass _____	coral _____
paint brush _____	seaweed _____
glue _____	paint box _____
book about the seashore _____	

Break the Paragraph, Dig for Details
Check Your Work

DIRECTIONS: Compare your work to the writer's. Did you break the article in the same place and figure out the main ideas of each paragraph?

Beach Art

If you get to the shore this summer, collect objects such as shells, seaweed, beach grass, tiny rocks, and driftwood. Next, look at illustrations of a beach to help you create a background. For the background you'll need heavy drawing paper or oak tag, paste and blue-green watercolors or felt-tip markers. Don't forget the newspapers to protect your floor or table.

Now you're ready to use your materials to paint a picture. Paint a sky and make a beach. Cover the bottom of the paper with paste and add sand. Use more paste to arrange the objects you've collected on the sand. Be sure to lay your beach art flat so the objects won't fall off. Your beach is complete. Just don't get a sunburn!

Main idea of paragraph 1: Preparing to create beach art

Main idea of paragraph 2: Creating beach art

Outline a Two-Paragraph
How-To Piece

DIRECTIONS: Select a craft, hobby, or activity that you can teach a friend. In two paragraphs, describe the preparation and procedures that your friend would need to do. Use this form to develop your ideas for each paragraph.

I will teach _____ how to_____

Topic or paragraph 1: _____

Opening sentence: _____

Preparation for your craft, hobby, or activity: _____

_____

_____

Topic or paragraph 2: _____

Opening sentence: _____

How to do your craft, hobby, or activity (steps, details, useful information):

_____

_____

A few final tips:_____

Closing sentence:_____

Reread your ideas carefully, looking for parts that aren't clear or could be improved and make whatever changes are needed.

THE ARTICLE'S PARAGRAPHS ¶ OPENING AND CLOSING PARAGRAPHS ¶ FOLLOWING TECHNIQUES STUDENT WRITERS USE ¶ WRITI
T'S THE PURPOSE OF EACH PARAGRAPH? ¶ DIALOGUE RULES ¶ UNTANGLE THE DIALOGUE ¶ WHO'S SAYING WHAT? ¶ SPEAKING OF
TING ASSIGNMENTS ¶ TEACHING PARAGRAPH BASICS ¶ EXPLORING THE PURPOSE OF PARAGRAPHS ¶ WHAT MAKES A PARAGRAPH
SING A PARAGRAPH WITH STRONG DETAILS ¶ WRITING TWO-PARAGRAPH PIECES ¶ STUDYING THE STRUCTURE OF A TWO-PARAG

MINI-LESSON

Writing a Two-Paragraph Book Report: Focus on Craft

INTRODUCTION: In my teaching, a problem typically arises at this point: Although most students can point out the form and content of a two-paragraph piece, few realize how those two elements work together to determine the piece's overall effectiveness. This lesson helps. It's designed to show students how to combine what they know about a paragraph's parts to craft well-written reports.

MATERIALS

- ☀ Individual copies and an overhead transparency of Student Activity 10 (page 39)
- ☀ Individual copies of Outline Guide 4: Two-Paragraph Book Report (page 45)

·············· SUGGESTIONS FOR TEACHING THE LESSON ···············

1 Begin the lesson by saying something like: "Writers are very careful about constructing two-paragraph pieces so that each paragraph is structured correctly *and* contains strong details. Let's look at two examples by students."

2 Show Activity 10A's Example 1, "The Caddis Fly" on the overhead, read it aloud, and distribute the individual copies.

3 Talk with students about how they might approach this assignment. Ask them to identify the parts of each paragraph: opening sentence, body sentences, and closing sentence.

4 Have students look closely at the writer's craft. Ask them:

- ☀ "What technique does the writer use to attract interest in the opening sentence?" Possible responses: "An interesting question…" "A wild thought…"
- ☀ "What do the body sentences' details describe?" Possible responses: "How the caddis worm builds its home…" "Where the caddis worm lives before it turns into a fly…"
- ☀ "Does the closing sentence sum up the topic and leave you satisfied? Why or why not?" Possible responses: "Yes, because it ends with the worm becoming a fly…" "No, the fly just flies away. What's the point?"

5 Repeat the lesson using Example 2, "An Important Change in James's Life."

6 Ask students to plan their own two-paragraph book report. Distribute copies of Outline Guide 4 to help them organize their thoughts.

Get Crafty With a Two-Paragraph Report

DIRECTIONS: The following science report should be written as two paragraphs because it contains more than one main idea. Read the report, find the sentence that introduces a new main idea, and place a paragraph mark (⌐) at that sentence. Then:

1. Underline the topic sentence of each paragraph.

2. Place brackets ([ ]) around the body sentences of each paragraph.

3. Underline the closing sentence or sentences of each paragraph.

Example 1:

The Caddis Fly

    Did you ever think of biting down your door? Well a caddis worm does. It makes a log like case when it's born. It makes the case from twigs, pebbles, and shells. It then pastes it together with saliva. It keeps two ends open, one for it to stick its head out and the other to stick its tail out. It builds this cage for protection and to camouflage itself. After a few months, the caddis worm starts to cover up the holes and change into a caddis fly. It bites down one of the walls with its powerful jaws. Then it crawls up a long plant and bursts out of the case, and flies away.

Write down why you think the topic sentence is or isn't good.

_____

_____

Name some of the details in the body sentences.

_____

_____

_____

What is the main idea of each paragraph? Think about what the details describe.

Main Idea #1:

_____

_____

_____

Main Idea #2:

_____

_____

_____

Do you think this is a good piece of writing? Why or why not?

_____

_____

_____

Now try it with this book report:

Example 2:

An Important Change in James's Life

    In the beginning of the book James was sad. He had two very mean aunts who hated him. He cleaned, cooked, washed and did work the aunts told him to do. They did not ask him to do the work. They made him do it. At the end, when he lived in the peach pit, he had all the playmates in the world. Many came to see James's famous home. The children asked him to tell his story again and again. So he wrote the story in the format of a book by R. Dahl.

STUDENT ACTIVITY 10A (cont.)

Write down why you think the topic sentence is or isn't good.

_____

_____

_____

Name some of the details in the body sentences.

_____

_____

_____

What is the main idea of each paragraph? Think about what the details describe.

Main Idea #1:

_____

_____

_____

Main Idea #2:

_____

_____

_____

Do you think this is a good piece of writing? Why or why not?

_____

_____

_____

Get Crafty With a Two-Paragraph Report
Check Your Work

DIRECTIONS: Compare your paragraph decisions to the writers'.

Example 1:

The Caddis Fly

Did you ever think of biting down your door? Well a caddis worm does. [It makes a log like case when it's born. It makes the case from twigs, pebbles, and shells. It then pastes it together with saliva. It keeps two ends open, one for it to stick its head out and the other to stick its tail out.] It builds this cage for protection and to camouflage itself.

After a few months, the caddis worm starts to cover up the holes and change into a caddis fly. [It bites down one of the walls with its powerful jaws.] Then it crawls up a long plant and bursts out of the case, and flies away.

Example 2:

An Important Change in James's Life

In the beginning of the book James was sad. He had two very mean aunts who hated him. [He cleaned, cooked, washed and did work the aunts told him to do.] They did not ask him to do the work. They made him do it.

At the end, when he lived in the peach pit, he had all the playmates in the world. [Many came to see James's famous home. The children asked him to tell his story again and again.] So he wrote the story in the format of a book by R. Dahl.

Break the Paragraph, Dig for Details, Part 2

DIRECTIONS: Each of the following book excerpts was written as two paragraphs, but they've been run together here. Read the excerpts, find the sentences that introduce a new main idea, and place a paragraph mark (⌐) at the start of those sentences. Then:

1 Underline the topic sentence of each paragraph.

2 Place brackets ([ ]) around the body of each paragraph.

3 Underline the closing sentence or sentences of each paragraph.

A. A terrible accident has transformed Billie Jo's life, scarring her inside and out. Her mother is gone. Her father can't talk about it. And the one thing that might make her feel better—playing the piano—is impossible with her wounded hands. To make matters worse, dust storms are devastating the family farm and all the farms nearby. While others flee from the dust bowl, Billie Jo is left to find peace in the bleak landscape of Oklahoma—and in the surprising landscape of her own heart.

From *Out of the Dust* by Karen Hesse (Scholastic)

B. One of the most interesting events of the twentieth century happened at Kitty Hawk, North Carolina, on December 17, 1903. Orville and Wilbur Wright flew in a flying machine for the first time. Only a few newspapers carried a story about it at the time—the others didn't believe it had really happened. Orville and Wilbur had always been interested in flight. They practiced building gliders until they understood all the principles of flight, and then they tried to find a gasoline engine for their plane. They finally had to build one. The longest flight they made that day was 852 feet.

From *Who Invented It and What Makes It Work?* by Sarah Leslie (Platt & Munk)

STUDENT ACTIVITY 11 (cont.)

Now that you've divided these excerpts into four paragraphs, take a close look at them. Which part of the paragraphs provides details?

_____

What is the main idea of each paragraph? Write what each paragraph's details describe.

Excerpt A:

Paragraph 1:_____

_____

Paragraph 2:_____

_____

List some of the details:

_____

_____

Excerpt B:

Paragraph 1:_____

_____

Paragraph 2:_____

_____

List some of the details:

_____

_____

Paragraph Power ○ Scholastic Professional Books

Name _____ Date _____

Outline a Two-Paragraph Book Report

DIRECTIONS:

1. Complete the form below to plan a two-paragraph description of a book you have read.

2. Use the outline to help you write your report. Be sure to use an opening sentence, body sentences, and a closing sentence for each paragraph.

Title and author of book: _____

Topic of paragraph 1: _____

Opening sentence: _____

Body sentences (details, examples, and descriptions that explain your topic):

_____

_____

_____

Closing sentence: _____

Topic of paragraph 2: _____

Opening sentence: _____

_____

Body sentences (details, examples, and descriptions that explain your topic):

_____

_____

_____

Closing sentence: _____

Name _____ Date _____

Writing Process Checklist

DIRECTIONS: Review your writing and check off what you've done.

Title of Report or Essay _____

In preparing this piece, I

1 wrote an outline for each paragraph in my report or essay. . . . . ☐

2 wrote a rough draft. . . . . ☐

3 wrote an attention-grabbing opening paragraph. . . . . ☐

4 included details that support each paragraph's main idea. . . . . ☐

5 wrote a closing paragraph that sums up my topic and will leave
   my reader satisfied. . . . . ☐

6 read the draft to my teacher or my writing partner and asked for
   suggestions about what I could add, change, or explain. . . . . ☐

7 checked my facts. . . . . ☐

8 tried to connect ideas in the closing sentence of a paragraph to the topic
   sentence of the paragraph that follows it. . . . . ☐

9 proofread my work to improve my paragraphs, sentences, word choices,
   grammar, and spellings. . . . . ☐

10 wrote a final copy. . . . . ☐

Paragraph Power ○ Scholastic Professional Books

PRIME TIME TO TEACH
PARAGRAPH
TRANSITIONS

IG A TWO-PARAGRAPH BOOK REPORT: FOCUS ON CRAFT ¶ PARAGRAPH TRANSITIONS ¶ [...] ¶ WRITING
HE ARTICLE'S PARAGRAPHS ¶ OPENING AND CLOSING PARAGRAPHS ¶ FOLLOWING TECHNIQUES STUDENT WRITERS USE ¶ WRITING
S THE PURPOSE OF EACH PARAGRAPH? ¶ DIALOGUE RULES ¶ UNTANGLE THE DIALOGUE ¶ WHO'S SAYING WHAT? ¶ SPEAKING OF P
G ASSIGNMENTS ¶ TEACHING PARAGRAPH BASICS ¶ EXPLORING THE PURPOSE OF PARAGRAPHS ¶ WHAT MAKES A PARAGRAPH A PA

MINI-LESSON

Writing Transitions

INTRODUCTION: For paragraphs to flow smoothly, transitional words, phrases, and sentences are essential. They are the glue that "sticks" ideas, actions, and events together. If your students are like mine, they're already using simple transitions such as "The next thing," "After that," "Later," and "And then..." to connect their paragraphs. This lesson will help them craft more effective ones.

MATERIALS

☀ Individual copies and an overhead transparency of Student Activities 12 (pages 50–51) and 13 (page 52)

·······SUGGESTIONS FOR TEACHING THE LESSON·······

1 Introduce the lesson by writing "transition" and "transportation" on the chalkboard or overhead. Ask students what the two words have in common. No doubt they'll notice that both words start with the prefix "trans." Ask them what they think "trans" might mean, based on other words they know that begin with it. Guide them toward understanding that it means "across," "beyond," or "through," and is usually associated with movement. Tell them, "A car moves us—or transports us—from one place to another. And a transition moves us from one idea to another. It tells the reader, 'I was talking about that, but now I'm going to be talking about something different.'"

2 Distribute Activity 12 and have students read Danny's report "Somewhere Out There."

3 Ask students to underline the final sentence of the first paragraph: "The flesh has decayed but the bones and imprints are left" and the opening sentences of the second paragraph: "Hundreds of years later a paleontologist notices a peculiar shape in the dirt. He dusts it off with a brush, slowly it takes the shape of bird."

4 Explain the paragraph transition, using the overhead transparency of the activity as a reference. Say something like: "Did you notice how Danny connects the last sentence of his first paragraph, about the stone bones and imprints of an ancient bird, to the first sentence of the second paragraph which describes their discovery a million years later? These connections between paragraphs are called transitions."

5 Continue this procedure on the other paragraphs in Danny's report.

6 Show students other examples of transitions, such as the book-cover summary from Activity 7 (page 27):

> Matilda is a genius. Unfortunately her family treats her like a dolt. Her crooked car salesman father and loud, bingo-obsessed mother think Matilda's only talent is as a scapegoat for everything that goes wrong in their miserable lives. But it's not too long before the sweet and sensitive child decides to fight back. Faced with practical jokes of sheer brilliance, her parents don't stand a chance.
>
> "The Trunchbull," however, is a different story. Miss Trunchbull, ex-Olympic hammer thrower and headmistress of Matilda's school, has terrorized generations of Crunchem Hall students—and teachers. But when she goes after sweet Miss Honey, the one teacher who believes in Matilda, she goes too far.

7 Have students look for transitions in books they are reading and share their findings. Tell them to be aware of words and phrases that signal a transition, such as "The next," "After that," "A week later," "Another way," "Soon," and "Also." Provide paper strips to mark the pages.

8 Have students copy the sentences that begin and end each transition, using Activity 12 as a guide, and share them with classmates. For extra practice, hand out Activity 13.

9 Encourage students to use transitions in their own writing.

STUDENT ACTIVITY **12**

Track the Report's Transitions

DIRECTIONS: Read the following report and underline the last sentence in the first paragraph and the opening sentences in the second paragraph. Then answer the questions that follow the report.

Somewhere Out There

by Danny, grade 5

A dead bird falls from the nest into the mud. One million years later, the mud has hardened. The minerals have gone into the tiny crevices of the bone, and turned the bone into stone! The flesh has decayed but the bones and imprints are left.

Hundreds of years later a paleontologist notices a peculiar shape in the dirt. He dusts it off with a brush, slowly it takes the shape of a bird. The paleontologist cuts around the imprint. He takes it out of the ground and wraps it in soft material and brings it to a laboratory to be analyzed. One of the methods to find out how old something is, is by counting the layers of dirt and rock around it.

Lots of animals and insects got stuck in sap, ice, and even tar. If something was frozen in ice at a cold enough temperature, it would not have decayed. It would be dead, but a bird or any other creature would be perfectly kept in ice. There have been cases when dinosaurs have been found preserved in ice or tar, and insects have even been found in sap.

Here's an example of the way sap preserved an insect. Almost a million years ago, a fly was buzzing around. It landed on some sap from a tree and got stuck. More sap piled onto it until it was covered. Then the sap hardened. A few years ago a team of paleontologists found this fossil. It was perfectly preserved.

STUDENT ACTIVITY 12 (cont.)

Notice how the last sentence in the first paragraph, which describes bones and imprints left in the dirt, is connected to the first sentences in the second paragraph, which describe their discovery hundreds of years later. This connection between paragraphs is called a *transition*.

- ☀ Last sentence of paragraph one: "The flesh has decayed but the bones and imprints are left."

- ☀ First sentences in paragraph two: "Hundreds of years later a paleontologist notices a peculiar shape in the dirt. He dusts it off with a brush, slowly it takes the shape of a bird."

1 One easy way to create a transition between paragraphs is to repeat a word or words that appeared in the last sentence of the previous paragraph. Can you find an example of this strategy in Danny's report? Underline the words he repeated. Which paragraphs did Danny connect by repeating words? Paragraphs ___ and ___.

2 Read the third and fourth paragraphs in Danny's report to find another example of transition sentences. Copy the sentences on the lines below and identify the strategy he used.

Transition sentence from paragraph 3:

_____

Transition sentence from paragraph 4:

_____

What strategy did Danny use to make the transition smooth?

_____

_____

_____

STUDENT ACTIVITY **13**

Look to Books for Transitions

DIRECTIONS: Scan a novel you've read recently for an example of a transition between two paragraphs. Look for words and phrases that signal a shift in ideas, actions, events, or speakers, such as "First," "Next," "After that," and "Later." On the lines below, copy the sentences that create the transition.

The final sentence of a paragraph:

_____

_____

_____

_____

The opening sentence of the paragraph that follows:

_____

_____

_____

What strategy did the writer use to make the transition smooth?

_____

_____

_____

TIPS FOR SHARPENING YOUR PARAGRAPH WRITING

* Read each paragraph in your piece and ask yourself: What is the main topic of this paragraph? Which details relate to the topic and which do not? Cut or move details that don't belong.

* If you see two different topics within the same paragraph, separate them using the paragraph editing mark (⌐).

* Begin each new paragraph with a transition, such as "first," "next," "after that," or "later," to signal to your reader that you are introducing a new idea, action, event, or speaker.

* Revise and recopy your piece, if necessary. Read it aloud to your teacher or a classmate, asking if any ideas are unclear or any information is missing. Also, keep in mind that unnecessarily long paragraphs often discourage readers. Keep yours short, if possible.

PART THREE

WRITING THREE-PARAGRAPH PIECES

NG A TWO-PARAGRAPH BOOK REPORT: FOCUS ON CRAFT ¶ PARAGRAPH TRANSITIONS ¶ WRITING THREE PARAGRAPH PIECES ¶ W
THE ARTICLE'S PARAGRAPHS ¶ OPENING AND CLOSING PARAGRAPHS ¶ FOLLOWING TECHNIQUES STUDENT WRITERS USE ¶ WRITIN
'S THE PURPOSE OF EACH PARAGRAPH? ¶ DIALOGUE RULES ¶ UNTANGLE THE DIALOGUE ¶ WHO'S SAYING WHAT? ¶ SPEAKING OF
NG ASSIGNMENTS ¶ TEACHING PARAGRAPH BASICS ¶ EXPLORING THE PURPOSE OF PARAGRAPHS ¶ WHAT MAKES A PARAGRAPH A

MINI-LESSON 10

Analyzing Three-Paragraph Reports

INTRODUCTION: Once your students have learned to write individual paragraphs containing topic, body, and closing sentences, and link them with smooth transitions, they can move on to more sophisticated pieces—pieces with three paragraphs, each with a distinct main idea. This lesson puts my students on the road to writing such pieces. It can do the same for yours.

MATERIALS

* Individual copies of Student Activities 14A (page 57), 15 (page 59), 16 (page 61), and 17 (page 63)
* Overhead of Student Activity 14B (page 58)
* Individual copies of the Self-Assessment Checklist 3 (page 79) to help students edit their writing

·············· SUGGESTIONS FOR TEACHING THE LESSON ················

1 Distribute Activity 14A, and show students how the book report "Amazing Fossils" presents three main ideas. Ask students to read the report to themselves and insert marks (⌐) to show where new paragraphs should begin. Point out that, if they were rewriting the paragraphs, they would break the lines and indent the sentence that follows these marks.

2 Show the 14B overhead transparency. Have students check their work and identify the main idea of each paragraph. Possible responses:

Paragraph 1: Tells what a fossil is and provides an example.

Paragraph 2: Describes three ways that fossils are formed.

Paragraph 3: Draws a conclusion. By testing and studying fossils, scientists can learn about the past.

3 For extra practice, hand out Activities 15, 16, and/or 17.

4 Connect the lesson to your curriculum. Have students write a three-paragraph report about a topic they are studying in math, history, or science. Remind them to begin with an outline. Distribute the checklist on page 79 to help them edit their work.

Name _____ Date _____

Edit a Science Report

DIRECTIONS: The report below was written by a fifth grader. It contains three main ideas and, therefore, should be broken into three paragraphs. Using paragraph marks (⌐), show where each new paragraph should begin.

Amazing Fossils

    Have you ever thought about fossils? A fossil is a trace or an imprint of a plant or animal that lived long ago. There are several different ways for a fossil to be formed. The mammoth was found in frozen grounds. When it was found it had some grass that it had eaten while it was still alive in its mouth! Some of the other ways for fossils to be formed are when a plant or animal dies, its bones get stuck in sap, and the sap preserves them. Fossils are also formed by the mud that covers them, and over the years sometimes, the mud preserves them until a paleontologist finds them. Paleontologists study the fossils very carefully. They put them through tests to find out how old they are. After they get all the clues, they make inferences on how the animal or plant looked and lived. Fossils can be helpful because scientists can learn about the past from fossils.

STUDENT ACTIVITY **14B**

Edit a Science Report
Check Your Work

DIRECTIONS: Compare your work to the writer's. Did you break the report in the same places?

Amazing Fossils

Have you ever thought about fossils? A fossil is a trace or an imprint of a plant or animal that lived long ago. There are several different ways for a fossil to be formed. The mammoth was found in frozen grounds. When it was found it had some grass that it had eaten while it was still alive in its mouth!

Some of the other ways for fossils to be formed are when a plant or animal dies, its bones get stuck in sap, and the sap preserves them. Fossils are also formed by the mud that covers them, and over the years sometimes, the mud preserves them until a paleontologist finds them.

Paleontologists study the fossils very carefully. They put them through tests to find out how old they are. After they get all the clues, they make inferences on how the animal or plant looked and lived. Fossils can be helpful because scientists can learn about the past from fossils.

Identify the topic of each paragraph. Write your ideas on the lines below.

Main idea of the opening paragraph: _____

Main idea of the body paragraph: _____

Main idea of the closing paragraph: _____

Reread the last sentence of the body paragraph and first sentence of the closing paragraph. Notice how they are connected. The last sentence of the body paragraph introduces the word "paleontologist" which is the main idea of the closing paragraph. What term do we use to identify that connection between paragraphs? _____

Name _____ Date _____

Edit a History Report

DIRECTIONS: The report below contains three main ideas and, therefore, should be broken into three paragraphs. Using the paragraph symbol (⌐⌐), show where each new paragraph should begin.

Gathering Wild Rice

Did you know the Indians were using wild rice way before Columbus discovered America in 1492? Columbus discovered the stalks and called them wild oats. The Indian women were the ones who did all the work. First the Indian women took a canoe to the river and paddled to the stalks of wild rice. Then they broke the stalks with a special sharp rock. Finally, they tied the stalks of rice together to keep the birds from eating the buds on the stalk. They had to wait for a month until the wild rice was ready to eat. In the fall, the Indian women cooked the wild rice for their families. Now wild rice is a delicacy in some parts of America. It grows on the edge of lakes or ponds. The wild rice stalk grows to about five to ten feet. Wild rice can be found from Virginia to Maine and especially in Wisconsin and Minnesota. If you want to taste wild rice, you might find it in the supermarket.

Write the main idea of each paragraph on the lines below.

Paragraph 1:_____

_____

Paragraph 2:_____

_____

Paragraph 3:_____

_____

Edit a History Report
Check Your Work

DIRECTIONS: Compare your work to the writer's. Did you break the report in the same places?

Gathering Wild Rice

Did you know that the Indians were using wild rice long before Columbus discovered America in 1492? Columbus discovered the stalks and called them wild oats.

The Indian women were the ones who did all the work. First the Indian women took a canoe to the river and paddled to the stalks of wild rice. Then they broke the stalks with a special sharp rock. Finally, they tied the stalks of rice together to keep the birds from eating the buds on the stalk. They had to wait for a month until the wild rice was ready to eat. In the fall, the Indian women cooked the wild rice for their families.

Now wild rice is a delicacy in some parts of America. It grows on the edge of lakes or ponds. The wild rice stalk grows to about five to ten feet. Wild rice can be found from Virginia to Maine and especially in Wisconsin and Minnesota. If you want to taste wild rice, you might find it in the supermarket.

Paragraph 1: Tells that Indians ate wild rice before Columbus came to America.

Paragraph 2: Describes how Indian women gathered and prepared wild rice.

Paragraph 3: Explains where wild rice grows today.

Edit a Book Report

DIRECTIONS:

1 Read the student book report below. Use the paragraph mark (⌐|) to show where a new topic begins and, therefore, a new paragraph should begin.

2 Put brackets ([ ]) around the topic sentence or sentences of each paragraph. Example: "[It was my aunt's wedding day and she looked beautiful.]"

3 Underline the details that support each topic. Example: "The bride wore a white, silk dress with a pink ribbon around her waist. Her veil was attached to flowers in her hair."

Leslie Burke from *Bridge to Terabithia* and Carlie from *The Pinballs* are two very different characters. One of Leslie's main problems is that she just moved and it's hard for her to adjust to her new surroundings. She doesn't even have a TV to watch! But Leslie does have a wonderful imagination which she uses to create an imaginary place called Terabithia. Leslie makes friends because she is a very caring person. Even though her best friend is a boy, she feels the same about Jess as she would about a best friend who is a girl. Carlie is a whole different story. She likes to think about reality, not fantasy. Carlie watches TV as much as she can. That's half the reason she doesn't have a good imagination. Carlie also doesn't adapt to changes well because it is hard for her to adjust to new surroundings and to make friends. For example, when she first came to the Mason's house, she was as rude as she could be to Mrs. Mason. Even though they are different, I think Leslie and Carlie could become good friends. Leslie could show Carlie how to use her imagination, and Carlie could teach Leslie what the real world is like and why it's important to be realistic sometimes.

Edit a Book Report
Check Your Work

DIRECTIONS: Compare your work to the writer's. Did you break the report in the same places and underline the same details?

[Leslie Burke from *Bridge to Terabithia* and Carlie from *The Pinballs* are two very different characters. One of Leslie's main problems is that she just moved and it's hard for her to adjust to her new surroundings.] She doesn't even have a TV to watch! But Leslie does have a wonderful imagination which she uses to create an imaginary place called Terabithia. Leslie makes friends because she is a very caring person. Even though her best friend is a boy, she feels the same about Jess as she would about a best friend who is a girl.

[Carlie is a whole different story. She likes to think about reality, not fantasy.] Carlie watches TV as much as she can. That's half the reason she doesn't have a good imagination. Carlie also doesn't adapt to changes well because it is hard for her to adjust to new surroundings and to make friends. For example, when she first came to the Mason's house, she was as rude as she could be to Mrs. Mason.

[Even though they are different, I think Leslie and Carlie could become good friends.] Leslie could show Carlie how to use her imagination, and Carlie could teach Leslie what the real world is like and why it's important to be realistic sometimes.

Write a Three-Paragraph Book Blurb

DIRECTIONS:

1. Look for good examples of back-cover summaries on paperback novels in your classroom or school library.

2. Choose a book you're reading or have read recently and write a three-paragraph back-cover summary for it, following the guidelines below.

Paragraph 1: Introduce the setting and the story's main character.

Paragraph 2: Describe the problem that the main character faces. Provide just enough details about the story problem to grab a reader's interest—but don't give away too much!

Paragraph 3: Write a closing paragraph. End your summary with a question or a statement that will make someone want to read the novel.

Title of Book: _____   Author: _____

_____

_____

_____

_____

_____

_____

_____

_____

_____

_____

_____

ING A TWO-PARAGRAPH BOOK REPORT: FOCUS ON CRAFT ¶ PARAGRAPH TRANSITIONS ¶ WRITING THREE-PARAGRAPH PIECES ¶ W
THE ARTICLE'S PARAGRAPHS ¶ OPENING AND CLOSING PARAGRAPHS ¶ FOLLOWING TECHNIQUES STUDENT WRITERS USE ¶ WRITI
T'S THE PURPOSE OF EACH PARAGRAPH? ¶ DIALOGUE RULES ¶ UNTANGLE THE DIALOGUE ¶ WHO'S SAYING WHAT? ¶ SPEAKING O
TING ASSIGNMENTS ¶ TEACHING PARAGRAPH BASICS ¶ EXPLORING THE PURPOSE OF PARAGRAPHS ¶ WHAT MAKES A PARAGRAPH

MINI-LESSON

Writing an Outline for a Three-Paragraph Report

INTRODUCTION: You and I, as teachers, know that planning is everything. And it's just as important for young writers. After your students have learned to write one- and two-paragraph pieces, and have looked closely at three-paragraph pieces, it will be easier for them to write longer pieces on their own if they begin with an outline. In this lesson, you'll show students the advantages of outlining before they begin writing.

MATERIALS

☀ Examples of student outlines on photocopies or overhead transparencies, including the one on page 65

☀ Individual copies and overhead transparency of one or more of the Outline Guides in this book. You'll find them on pages 23, 31, 37, 45, 67, 73, and 75.

☀ Individual copies of Student Activity 18 (page 66)

.... SUGGESTIONS FOR TEACHING THE LESSON...............

1 Show students examples of outlines, using photocopies or transparencies on the overhead projector. Help them to see how an outline is a powerful tool to help writers organize their thinking.

2 Distribute Student Activity 18 and have students complete it.

3 Tell students to select a topic that they are interested in and know a lot about. For example, a subject they have studied, a school activity, a class trip, or a special interest such as stamp collecting, model building, baseball, or tennis.

4 Before they write, have them think about how they can organize their topic into "parcels" that will make it easier for a reader to follow. Each parcel will become a paragraph.

5 Ask them to write the outline. Once students have thought of main ideas for each paragraph, they can list the ideas on paper, leaving several blank lines between each one for notes about the details they plan to use in developing each paragraph.

   Students can also use the Outline Guides that appear throughout this book for various kinds of writing tasks.

SAMPLE OUTLINE FOR A HISTORY REPORT

TOPIC: The Boston Tea Party

PARAGRAPH 1: Bad relations between England and colonies

- ☀ England had no money after the French and Indian War

- ☀ Imposed heavy taxes on tea—colonists' favorite drink

PARAGRAPH 2: Trouble begins

- ☀ Nov. 18, 1773—ship with tea sails into Boston Harbor

- ☀ Colonists had no money to pay tax, told English captain to go back

- ☀ England sends more ships sets deadline for unloading tea

- ☀ 7000 colonists and Sam Adams get mad, want to dump the tea overboard: "Boston Harbor will be a teapot tonight."

PARAGRAPH 3: Colonists dress up like Indians

- ☀ Dump the tea into the water

- ☀ They win with no fighting or violence

See the student's three-paragraph report, based on the outline, in the activity on the next page.

Match the Main Idea to the Paragraph

DIRECTIONS: Read the following student history report and identify each paragraph's main idea.

The Boston Tea Party

  The good relations between the colonies and their mother country, England, began to break down after the long bitter French and Indian war. Britain was in great debt, so they imposed heavy taxes on the colonies. Tea was the Americans' favorite drink. For this reason, the tax on tea was hard to pay.

The main idea is _____

  On November 18, 1773 the tea ship, Dartmouth, sailed into Boston Harbor. Townspeople demanded that the ship be sent directly back to England. As the days passed two more ships came. Tension came to all of Boston. Finally the governor set a deadline. He ordered the Dartmouth to be reloaded by December 17, 1773.

The main idea is _____

  At the largest mass meeting in Boston's history, on the evening of December 16, seven thousand people gathered at Boston's Old South Meeting House. Many speeches were delivered against taxes while the crowd's mood was angry. Sam Adams took the floor and said, "the Boston Harbor will be a teapot tonight!" Hundreds of townspeople disguised as Mohawk Indians stormed out of the meeting hall to dump the tea into the harbor. And, without any violence, they succeeded brilliantly.

The main idea is _____

Now connect the main idea to the appropriate paragraph.

Main Idea	Paragraph Number
A. Colonists force English tea ships to turn back.	_____
B. Boston townspeople refuse to pay taxes on English tea.	_____
C. England taxes tea.	_____

Paragraph Power ○ Scholastic Professional Books

Name _____ Date_____

Outline a Three-Paragraph Report

DIRECTIONS: Think about a topic in science, history, or current events that interests you. If you already have an assigned report on a particular topic, you're in luck. This form will get you off to a great start.

Topic:_____

Main idea of paragraph 1: _____

Opening sentence: _____

_____

Body sentences (list details, descriptions, examples that support the main idea):

_____

_____

_____

_____

_____

Transition sentence that leads to next main idea:

_____

_____

Main idea of paragraph 2: _____

Opening sentence: _____

_____

(cont.)

Body sentences (list details, descriptions, examples that support the main idea):

_____

_____

_____

Transition sentence that leads to the next main idea:

_____

_____

Main idea of paragraph 3: _____

Opening sentence: _____

_____

Body sentences (list details, descriptions, examples that support the main idea):

_____

_____

_____

_____

Transition sentence that leads to the closing:_____

_____

Closing sentence(s):

_____

_____

Paragraph Power ○ Scholastic Professional Books

MINI-LESSON

Analyzing a Three-Paragraph Article and Essay

INTRODUCTION: I often tell my students that being able to organize and craft paragraphs isn't important only in the classroom. It's important in the real world, too. This lesson helps you show students how professional writers compose three-paragraph articles for children's magazines.

MATERIALS

☀ Individual copies and an overhead transparency of Student Activities 19 (page 70) and 20 (page 72)

···············SUGGESTIONS FOR TEACHING THE LESSON···············

1 Begin by telling students something like: "News articles follow paragraphing rules. They have an opening paragraph, one or more body paragraphs, a closing paragraph, and smooth transitions throughout. Each paragraph is indented. Professional writers build their paragraphs with details that help readers 'see' what is happening."

2 Distribute Activity 19 and show the overhead transparency. Have students find the paragraphs in the article, "Catch a Falling Star," according to the directions.

3 Ask students to identify the main idea of each paragraph. Possible responses:

☀ "Paragraph one connects fireworks to our past experiences on the Fourth of July."

☀ "Paragraph two introduces the main topic, meteor showers, by comparing them to fireworks."

4 Repeat the lesson using Activity 20, based on a three-paragraph essay.

5 Connect the lesson to your social studies curriculum. Have students write a three-paragraph news article in the present tense, reporting on an historical event. Encourage them to use descriptions, details, and quotations that make the event appear to have happened recently.

Name _____ Date _____

Find the Article's Paragraphs

DIRECTIONS: The short article below contains two main ideas and, therefore, should be broken into two paragraphs. Use paragraph marks (⌐) to separate the paragraphs. Underline the opening and closing sentences of each paragraph.

Catch a Falling Star

by Robert Irion

Everybody loves fireworks. Colorful explosions fill the air as you lie on the grass, still stuffed from your Fourth of July barbecue. It's a perfect way to end the holiday. The night sky also provides its own fireworks, and you don't have to wait until next July 4 to see them. In fact, August is the best month to see a meteor shower, one of nature's most beautiful sky shows. Watching a meteor shower is easy and fun. All you need are your eyes, a clear night, and some time.

From *Highlights for Children*

Now try it with this student's article:

Computers Help Us a Lot

by Robbie, grade 4

What do these words remind you of: software, disks, hard drives, monitor, keyboard, modem, tower, central processing unit? Well here's another clue. It can help you with just about everything you do in school. It's a computer! Our class is working on two programs. They are Logo Writer and Odell Lake. Logo Writer is a disk that helps us with geometry. Logo Writer has everything. It even can help us make music. Odell Lake helps us learn about pond life, a unit we are studying in science. We work in the computer room with Mr. Gaskin our special computer teacher on Tuesdays and Thursdays for 45 minutes. These two programs are fun to do and everyone in our class always likes using them.

Paragraph Power ○ Scholastic Professional Books

STUDENT ACTIVITY **19B**

Find the Article's Paragraphs
Check Your Work

DIRECTIONS: Compare your work to the writers'. Did you break the articles in the same places and underline the opening and closing sentences of each paragraph?

Catch a Falling Star

by Robert Irion

   Everybody loves fireworks. Colorful explosions fill the air as you lie on the grass, still stuffed from your Fourth of July barbecue. It's a perfect way to end the holiday.

   The night sky also provides its own fireworks, and you don't have to wait until next July 4 to see them. In fact, August is the best month to see a meteor shower, one of nature's most beautiful sky shows. Watching a meteor shower is easy and fun. All you need are your eyes, a clear night, and some time.

From *Highlights for Children*

Computers Help Us a Lot

by Robbie, grade 4

   What do these words remind you of: software, disks, hard drives, monitor, keyboard, modem, tower, central processing unit? Well here's another clue. It can help you with just about everything you do in school. It's a computer!

   Our class is working on two programs. They are Logo Writer and Odell Lake. Logo Writer is a disk that helps us with geometry. Logo Writer has everything. It even can help us make music. Odell Lake helps us learn about pond life, a unit we are studying in science. We work in the computer room with Mr. Gaskin our special computer teacher on Tuesdays and Thursdays for 45 minutes. These two programs are fun to do and everyone in our class always likes using them.

Find the Essay's Main Ideas

DIRECTIONS: Break the following short essay into three paragraphs. Then reread it to identify the main idea of each paragraph.

Chocolate World

Learning about chocolate was delicious! The first thing we saw at Chocolate World was what the old chocolate wrappers looked like. They weren't as shiny as the wrappers are today. Then we got in a little car that moved on a circular floor and we saw how they mixed the liquid chocolate and poured it into molds. It looked so good you just felt like sticking your finger in and licking it. Before I went to Hershey, I really never knew much about chocolate. Not only did we see how chocolate was made, but we also bought plenty of samples.

What do the sentences in each paragraph describe? Write their main ideas below.

Main idea of the opening paragraph: _____

_____

_____

Main idea of the body paragraph: _____

_____

_____

Main idea of the closing paragraph: _____

_____

_____

Paragraph Power ○ Scholastic Professional Books

Outline GUIDE 6

Outline a
Three-Paragraph Article

DIRECTIONS: Be a news reporter. Think of a school activity or project that you could write up in three paragraphs. Use this form below to plan your article.

Name the activity or project: _____

Opening Paragraph

How will you introduce the topic to grab a reader's interest?

_____

_____

_____

Body Paragraph

Make notes of details or information that the body paragraph will include. You can interview people to get information.

_____

_____

_____

_____

_____

Closing Paragraph

How will you close your article? How will you leave your reader satisfied?

_____

_____

_____

Strategies for Sharing Drafts and Finished Pieces

My students always read aloud their works-in-progress, as well as their completed reports and essays, to their classmates, to get responses and suggestions. Here are some tips for planning a daily 10-minute sharing time.

- ☀ Post a sign-up sheet for students who want to share their writing and receive feedback. It's a good idea to ask each student who has signed up what kind of help he or she needs. This will help the listeners focus their feedback.

- ☀ If time is limited, have students read aloud only one part of their paper and summarize the rest.

- ☀ Encourage students to respond to their classmates' read-alouds by pointing out a part they liked, asking questions, and then offering suggestions. For example, "I liked the way you described your grandmother as a jolly, round lady. What kind of games did you play with her when you were sick? Maybe you could tell us more about them."

- ☀ Focus on specific aspects of craft. For example, have a student read only the opening and closing paragraphs. Then ask classmates to identify the technique he or she used for writing those paragraphs. (See pages 82 and 85 for mini-lessons on techniques for writing opening and closing paragraphs.)

Outline a Three-Paragraph Essay

DIRECTIONS: From the list below, choose a topic that interests you and that you know a lot about—and then plan your essay by filling out the form that follows.

A. Choose a topic.

a friend or relative	a big surprise	a sport you play or watch
your hobby	a humorous incident	a holiday celebration
an accident	a TV show or movie	a family pet
a special place	a great book	your own idea:_____

B. Plan your first paragraph.

Write your topic sentence or sentences on the lines below. Think about the one main idea that every detail in the paragraph will tell about.

_____

_____

List details that you will use to support the main idea of the paragraph.

_____

_____

Write a transition, one or two closing sentences that lead into the main idea of the second paragraph.

_____

_____

C. Plan your second paragraph.

Write your topic sentence or sentences on the lines below. Think about the one main idea that every detail in the paragraph will tell about.

_____

_____

(cont.)

Name _____ Date _____

List details that you will use to support the main idea of the paragraph.

_____

_____

Write a transition, one or two closing sentences that lead into the main idea of the third paragraph.

_____

_____

D. Plan your third paragraph.

Write your topic sentence or sentences on the lines below. Think about the one main idea that every detail in the paragraph will tell about.

_____

_____

List details that you will use to support the main idea of the paragraph.

_____

_____

E. Write one or two closing sentences for the essay.

_____

_____

_____

F. Think of a title that will grab your readers' interest.

_____

Paragraph Power ○ Scholastic Professional Books

FUN AND FAST THREE-PARAGRAPH WRITING ASSIGNMENTS

Here are some assignments for writing three-paragraph pieces that kids just love.

IDEA 1: Create a Story from a Comic Strip

Have students bring in comic strips (non-violent ones preferably) and turn them into three-paragraph stories, using as much action, description, and dialogue as necessary to convey their ideas well. It might be helpful to model this process for the whole class before students try it on their own. Be sure to see page 120 for tips on dialogue writing.

IDEA 2: Change a School Rule

Are there school rules your students aren't happy about? Let them plan a three-paragraph essay that argues for a change.

- ☀ In the first paragraph, students should describe the rule and tell why it should be changed, using specific details and examples.

- ☀ In the second paragraph, they should describe the changes they would like to see and suggest alternatives to the rule.

- ☀ In the third paragraph, they should sum up their argument effectively.

IDEA 3: Follow the Directions

Have students write directions for any of the following activities. Encourage them to be as serious or as zany as they like.

- ☀ How to play a game

- ☀ How to prepare your favorite recipe

- ☀ How to care for your pet while you're away

- ☀ How to do homework

- ☀ How to build a model

- ☀ How to write a letter

- ☀ How to get a babysitting job

(cont.)

EXAMPLES OF "FOLLOW THE DIRECTIONS" PIECES:

How to Make a Family-Picture Greeting Card

To make each greeting card, you will need the following materials: folded construction paper, colored felt-tip markers, scissors, a cut-out photo of the face of each member of your family, scissors, and paste.

On the front side of the folded construction paper, draw a house with a front door and enough windows to show the cut-out photos. Paste a photo in each window, and print the name of each person below the window.

Inside the card, write a message such as Happy Holiday, Get Well Soon, Congratulations, or use your own idea. Buy stamps and envelopes to fit your cards and address them. Now send each greeting card on its way!

How to Estimate an Answer to a Math Problem

Today we learned about front-ending. Front-ending is estimating. Why do we need it? Because 80% of math in people's lives is estimating.

$$
\begin{array}{r}
284 \\
1{,}400 \\
+\ \ \ 9{,}000 \\
\hline
\end{array}
$$

If you have that addition problem, you could add each column separately to get your answer. But if you wanted to get a good idea of your answer, you could do it in your head a faster way.

If you don't know what I mean, here is an example of front-ending. Focus on the numbers in the highest place value column. You add 9,000 and the 1,000 and you get 10,000. Now you have your estimated answer.

Paragraph Power ○ Scholastic Professional Books

General Editing Checklist

DIRECTIONS: Review your writing and check off what you've done.

Title of My Piece _____

1 Each body paragraph has

  a main idea. . . . . ☐

  a topic sentence. . . . . ☐

  supporting details . . . . ☐

  a closing sentence . . . . ☐

2 My first paragraph draws a reader's attention. . . . . ☐

3 My final paragraph wraps up the piece effectively. . . . . . ☐

4 I followed paragraph writing customs:

  I indented the first line of each paragraph. . . . . ☐

  I started a new paragraph for each speaker. . . . . ☐

  I used punctuation marks correctly. . . . . ☐

  I spelled all the words correctly. . . . . ☐

  I used capital letters appropriately. . . . . ☐

PRIME TIME TO TEACH
OPENING AND CLOSING PARAGRAPHS

NG A TWO PARAGRAPH BOOK REPORT. FOCUS ON CRAFT ¶ PARAGRAPH TRANSITIONS ¶ WRITIN
THE ARTICLE'S PARAGRAPHS ¶ OPENING AND CLOSING PARAGRAPHS ¶ FOLLOWING TECHNIQUES STUDENT WRITERS USE ¶ WRITIN
'S THE PURPOSE OF EACH PARAGRAPH? ¶ DIALOGUE RULES ¶ UNTANGLE THE DIALOGUE ¶ WHO'S SAYING WHAT? ¶ SPEAKING OF
ING ASSIGNMENTS ¶ TEACHING PARAGRAPH BASICS ¶ EXPLORING THE PURPOSE OF PARAGRAPHS ¶ WHAT MAKES A PARAGRAPH A

MINI-LESSON

Looking at Powerful Opening and Closing Sentences

INTRODUCTION: The first sentence of a report or essay serves two important purposes. It introduces the topic and the information that follows, and—if it is well written—persuades a reader to continue reading. The last sentence is equally important because, ideally, it leaves the reader with a sense of satisfaction. Students must be able to write first and last sentences effectively. This lesson always helps my students appreciate the qualities of strong openings and closings.

MATERIALS

☀ Individual copies and an overhead transparency of Student Activity 21 (pages 83–84)

············· SUGGESTIONS FOR TEACHING THE LESSON ···············

1 Introduce the lesson by saying something like: "Writers work hard to create effective opening and closing paragraphs. In your opinion, why are opening paragraphs particularly important?" Possible responses: "It tells you what the piece is about" and "If an opening paragraph isn't interesting, no one will want to read the rest of the piece."

2 Distribute Student Activity 21 and show it on the overhead. Say something like: "First read the piece labeled 'Example 1 (Draft)' and then read 'Example 2 (Revision)' to look for changes that the student made in her opening and closing paragraphs. Think about which example was more effective and easier to understand."

3 Have students fill out the checklist that follows the "before" and "after" paragraphs.

4 Discuss responses as a class. Ask students to explain why they chose one example instead of the other. Then offer your own ideas for choosing the "after" paragraph. For example, you might say something like: "The opening sentence of the first paragraph made me want to find out why this book was so 'great.' That lead caught my interest because I'm always looking for a good book to read.

"The word 'tragic' in the opening sentence of the second paragraph made me want to know more about Daphne's secret. I also want to find the answer to the question in the closing sentence. Does Jessica keep the secret or will she ask her teacher to help Daphne?"

STUDENT ACTIVITY **21**

Compare the "Before" and "After" Paragraphs

DIRECTIONS: Read the student's paragraph draft and revision, looking for changes that she made to improve her paragraphs. Answer the questions that follow.

Example 1 (Draft):

   I just finished a book called "Daphne's Book" by Mary Downing Hahn. In this story Jessica and Daphne are assigned to be partners for a Write-a-Book contest. Daphne is a new girl that everyone thinks is strange and Jessica doesn't really want to be her partner. But when Jessica gets to know Daphne, she gets to like her and trust her. Then Jessica finds out Daphne's tragic secret. If Jessica asks her teacher for help, Daphne might be mad that she told someone else the secret. It's up to Jessica to decide what she wants to save, either Daphne's friendship or Daphne, herself.

Example 2 (Revision):

   If you're looking for a great book, read *Daphne's Book* by Mary Downing Hahn. In this story, Jessica and Daphne are assigned to be partners for a Write-a-Book contest. Daphne is a new girl that everyone thinks is strange and Jessica doesn't really want to be her partner. But when Jessica gets to know Daphne, she gets to like her and trust her.

   Then Jessica finds out Daphne's tragic secret. If Jessica asks her teacher for help, Daphne might be mad that Jessica told someone else the secret. It's up to Jessica to decide what she wants to save, either Daphne's friendship or Daphne, herself. Read this book to find out what Jessica does.

Compare the Before and After examples on the first page. Answer the questions by writing "1" or "2" in the spaces following each one.

Which example shows:

two topics in one paragraph? _____

one topic in each paragraph? _____

a better opening sentence?   _____ Why?_____

_____

a better closing sentence?   _____ Why?_____

_____

On Your Own

Look for a "needy" paragraph in something you've written. Rewrite the paragraph. Then use the checklist above to compare your own "before" and "after" examples.

ITING A TWO-PARAGRAPH BOOK REPORT: FOCUS ON CRAFT ¶ PARAGRAPH TRANSITIONS ¶ WRITING THREE-PARAGRAPH PIECES ¶
ND THE ARTICLE'S PARAGRAPHS ¶ OPENING AND CLOSING PARAGRAPHS ¶ FOLLOWING TECHNIQUES STUDENT WRITERS USE ¶ WRIT
AT'S THE PURPOSE OF EACH PARAGRAPH? ¶ DIALOGUE RULES ¶ UNTANGLE THE DIALOGUE ¶ WHO'S SAYING WHAT? ¶ SPEAKING C
ITING ASSIGNMENTS ¶ TEACHING PARAGRAPH BASICS ¶ EXPLORING THE PURPOSE OF PARAGRAPHS ¶ WHAT MAKES A PARAGRAPH

MINI-LESSON 14

Following Techniques Student Writers Use

INTRODUCTION: Most writers, professionals and skilled amateurs, do not come up with effective leads as soon as they begin to write. They experiment by trying out various techniques and then choosing the best one to suit their audience.

I've found one of the best ways to get students experimenting with these techniques is to have them see and hear effective examples written by kids who have used them. This lesson will give your students plenty of inspiration.

MATERIALS

☀ Individual copies and an overhead transparency of Student Activity 22 (pages 86–87)

·············· SUGGESTIONS FOR TEACHING THE LESSON ···············

1 Write the following list on the chalkboard or on an overhead transparency.

Action	Question	Dialogue (spoken words or thoughts)
Interesting fact	Unusual image	Description

2 Introduce the lesson. Say something like: "An opening paragraph is like the first act of a play. If it's not interesting, people will leave before it's over. These are some of the techniques writers use to hook their audience and keep it reading."

3 Read aloud the following opening paragraphs and ask students to identify the technique or techniques each student writer used to grab the reader's attention.

A. The clock on our classroom wall showed three o'clock. I raced out of school and ran home as fast as I could. I was as free as a floating balloon. No homework, no spelling, no nothing. And it was my birthday! **Technique?**_____

B. The night air was still as about 200 men and boys dressed as Mohawk Indians hurried down back alleys towards three ships waiting in Boston Harbor. The names of these ships were the Dartmouth, the Beaver, and the Eleanor. Their cargo was tea, 342 boxes of tea all together. **Technique?**_____

4 Distribute Activity 22 and give students enough time to complete it.

5 Show the transparency of the activity and discuss responses as a class.

STUDENT ACTIVITY **22**

Name that Technique

DIRECTIONS: Students just like you wrote the following opening sentences. Read each sentence and determine the technique or techniques used to capture the reader's interest. Write the code(s) for the technique(s) on the lines following the sentences.

Codes: A = Action   D = Dialogue (spoken words or thoughts)

Q = Question   U = Unusual image

I = Interesting fact   S = Setting description

1 "The orange boat glided leisurely across the water. I watched the sail billowing out like a fat giant's belly. The sun beat on me soaking me in its rays." _____

From "The Breaks of Sailing" by Nathan, grade 6

2 "Yay! It's my birthday!" I squealed as I hopped out of bed and skipped down the hall. _____

From "Temporary Forgetfulness" by Dan, grade 4

3 "I shuffled slowly into the classroom gripping my mother's hand as tightly as I could. My knees were wobbling, I felt I might fall at any moment." _____

From "My First Day at Greenacres School" by Libby, grade 5

4 "Mom, have you seen Ernie?" I asked.
"Nope," she answered.
"Ernie, come on kitty," I called as I opened a can of cat food for her. _____

From "Ernie, Always and Forever" by Susie, grade 6

5 We came to a halt outside an animal store. I wandered inside looking at all kinds of fish, canaries, and cats. _____

From "The Special Birthday Gift" by Maria, grade 6

Paragraph Power ∘ Scholastic Professional Books

6 Tick, tick, tick, tick... tick... tick...."And the number is..." Everyone standing at the wheel of fortune booth at the Edgewood Fair on May seventh held their breaths. They stared at the kelly green and white wheel with the numbers one through 16 on it as it spun slower and slower. Their eyes were glued to the wheel. You could feel the mounting excitement. People bit their fingernails and cracked their knuckles. They paid no attention to the shrieks of laughter and noisy yells that came from the rest of the fair on the blacktop behind them.

_____

From "The Edgewood Fair,"
by Amy, grade 6

On Your Own

Look at several paragraphs in a book you are reading now to find an interesting opening sentence. Write the sentence or sentences on the lines below.

_____

_____

_____

_____

_____

_____

_____

MINI-LESSON 15

Analyzing Effective Opening and Closing Paragraphs

INTRODUCTION: Once my students have a grasp of basic techniques for opening paragraphs, I conduct this lesson with them. It nudges them toward using more advanced techniques such as surprising the reader, showing a feeling, or stating the resolution—techniques that skilled writers use for both opening and closing paragraphs.

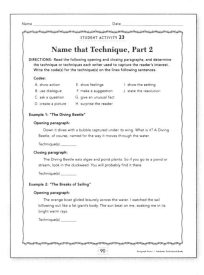
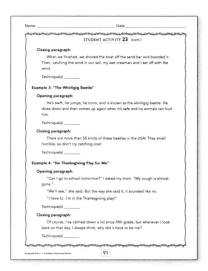

MATERIALS

☀ Individual copies of Student Activity 23 (pages 90–91)

· · · · · · · · · · · · · · **SUGGESTIONS FOR TEACHING THE LESSON** · · · · · · · · · · · · · ·

1 Write the following techniques writers use on a chart, chalkboard, or overhead transparency:

show action	create a picture	give an unusual fact
use dialogue	show feelings	surprise the reader
ask a question	make a suggestion	show the setting
state the resolution		

2 Introduce the lesson by saying something like: "Take a few minutes to read the variety of techniques that writers use to develop interesting opening and closing paragraphs."

3 Read aloud an example. Say something like: "Listen carefully as I read the opening and closing paragraphs in a student essay entitled 'A Soccer Game I'll Never Forget.'"

Opening paragraph:

"Dribble, Dave! Dribble!" I screamed. We were losing the soccer game 2-1 against Fox Meadow.

4 Ask students which two techniques the writer used. (Good answers: use dialogue and show action)

Closing paragraph:

I had tied up the score with 43 seconds left. I tried hard not to smile a lot because I thought everybody would think I was showing off. But it was hard not to smile because I was happy.

5 Ask students which two techniques the writer used. (Answer: states resolution and shows feelings)

6 Distribute Activity 23 to give students additional practice in identifying techniques. Possible responses:

Opening Paragraph	Closing Paragraph
1. A, C	F
2. D, I	D, J
3. A	G
4. B, C	C, E

Follow It Up

Follow up the lesson by having students read aloud examples of effective opening and closing paragraphs in their own writings and in the books they're reading. Have the class identify the techniques the writers used.

Name that Technique, Part 2

DIRECTIONS: Read the following opening and closing paragraphs, and determine the technique or techniques each writer used to capture the reader's interest. Write the code(s) for the technique(s) on the lines following sentences.

Codes:

A. show action	E. show feelings	I. show the setting
B. use dialogue	F. make a suggestion	J. state the resolution
C. ask a question	G. give an unusual fact	
D. create a picture	H. surprise the reader	

Example 1: "The Diving Beetle"

Opening paragraph:

Down it dives with a bubble captured under its wing. What is it? A Diving Beetle, of course, named for the way it moves through the water.

Technique(s) _____

Closing paragraph:

The Diving Beetle eats algae and pond plants. So if you go to a pond or stream, look in the duckweed. You will probably find it there.

Technique(s) _____

Example 2: "The Breaks of Sailing"

Opening paragraph:

The orange boat glided leisurely across the water. I watched the sail billowing out like a fat giant's body. The sun beat on me, soaking me in its bright warm rays.

Technique(s) _____

Paragraph Power ◦ Scholastic Professional Books

Closing paragraph:

When we finished, we shoved the boat off the sand bar and boarded it. Then, catching the wind in our sail, my wet crewman and I set off with the wind.

Technique(s) _____

Example 3: "The Whirligig Beetle"

Opening paragraph:

He's swift, he jumps, he turns, and is known as the whirligig beetle. He dives down and then comes up again when it's safe and no animals can hurt him.

Technique(s) _____

Closing paragraph:

There are more than 50 kinds of these beetles in the USA! They smell horrible, so don't try catching one!

Technique(s) _____

Example 4: "No Thanksgiving Play for Me"

Opening paragraph:

"Can I go to school tomorrow?" I asked my mom. "My cough is almost gone."

"We'll see," she said. But the way she said it, it sounded like no.

"I have to. I'm in the Thanksgiving play!"

Technique(s) _____

Closing paragraph:

Of course, I've calmed down a lot since fifth grade, but whenever I look back on that day, I always think, why did it have to be me?

Technique(s) _____

PART FOUR

WRITING MULTI-PARAGRAPH REPORTS AND ESSAYS

ING A TWO-PARAGRAPH BOOK REPORT: FOCUS ON CRAFT ¶ PARAGRAPH TRANSITIONS ¶ WRITING THREE-PARAGRAPH PIECES ¶ W
D THE ARTICLE'S PARAGRAPHS ¶ OPENING AND CLOSING PARAGRAPHS ¶ FOLLOWING TECHNIQUES STUDENT WRITERS USE ¶ WRITI
T'S THE PURPOSE OF EACH PARAGRAPH? ¶ DIALOGUE RULES ¶ UNTANGLE THE DIALOGUE ¶ WHO'S SAYING WHAT? ¶ SPEAKING O
TING ASSIGNMENTS ¶ TEACHING PARAGRAPH BASICS ¶ EXPLORING THE PURPOSE OF PARAGRAPHS ¶ WHAT MAKES A PARAGRAPH A

Using Book Blurbs to Improve Multi-Paragraph Writing

INTRODUCTION: As students move up the grades, writing demands become heavier. They're expected to understand grammar, mechanics, and the composing process well enough to write full-fledged, multi-paragraph essays and reports in all subject areas. This can be daunting. So start them out with something familiar.

As I mentioned earlier, my students read the back-cover summaries on paperback books to see if a story interests them. These summaries are excellent models of effective multi-paragraph writing. Here's a way to get students thinking about how and why they are effective.

MATERIALS

☀ Individual copies of Student Activities 24 (page 95), 25 (page 96), 26 (page 100), and 27 (page 102)

⋯⋯⋯⋯⋯⋯ SUGGESTIONS FOR TEACHING THE LESSON ⋯⋯⋯⋯⋯⋯

1 Distribute copies of Activity 24 and say something like: "Read the paragraphs from the back cover summary of *The Midnight Fox* by Betsy Byars. Notice how each paragraph, though brief, presents its topic effectively."

2 Focus on the writer's craft—for example, her use of the present tense. Ask, "Why do you think the writer of this back cover summary used the present tense?" Possible responses: "It makes things feel like they're taking place before our eyes," "To make us feel that it's happening now," and "It's like we're watching a show on TV."

3 Talk about each paragraph's purpose—the fact that the first and second paragraphs primarily introduce the setting and main character, and the third and fourth paragraphs focus on the main character's problem.

4 Look at the technique the writer used in the opening and closing paragraphs. Say something like: "The writing shows something else that's interesting. Did you notice that the writer began and ended the summary with a question? Why would a writer do that?" Possible responses: "To make you want to find out what happens" and "To get someone to read the book and find the answer."

5 For extra practice, hand out Activities 25, 26, and/or 27.

What's Each Paragraph's Purpose?

DIRECTIONS: Read the following back-cover summary for *The Midnight Fox* by Betsy Byars.

> Who wants to spend the summer on a stupid farm? Tom sure doesn't! But he has to stay with his aunt and uncle while his parents are away.
>
> The farm is boring, just as Tom knew it would be—until he sees the fox. She is wild and graceful, and black as midnight. Tom spends all his time in the woods, watching for her, even tracking down her den.
>
> But when she steals Aunt Millie's turkey, Uncle Fred vows to kill the fox. And he cages her little cub to lure the fox to her death.
>
> Now it's up to Tom. Can he save the beautiful fox and her cub—before his uncle kills them?

1 Determine the main ideas:

Paragraphs 1 and 2 focus on: _____

Paragraphs 3 and 4 focus on: _____

2 Reread the opening sentences of paragraph 1. How does the writer capture a reader's interest?

_____

3 Reread the closing sentence of the final paragraph. How does the final sentence create suspense?

_____

_____

_____

Report on the Reports' Paragraphs

DIRECTIONS: The reports below contain multiple main ideas and, therefore, should be broken into multiple paragraphs. Using the paragraph mark (⌐), show where each new paragraph should begin.

Use three paragraph marks:

The Foster Parent Plan

The cowbird is a "nest parasite." It lays its eggs in the nests of other birds. Cardinals are common victims of the cowbird in Florida, as are red-winged blackbirds and many other species. The cowbird is the only land bird in the United States with this trait. Most of the birds chosen as foster parents will tolerate the extra egg and treat the hatchling as one of their own. However, cowbird eggs hatch quickly and the baby cowbird frequently out-grows and out-eats the offspring of the host birds. The cowbird chick is often the only survivor. Not all birds will accept a cowbird egg laid in their nest. The birds of some species will remove the egg, some will abandon or rebuild the nest, and some will even build another nest layer right on top of the cowbird egg.

From *Florida's Fabulous Birds*
by Winston Williams (World Publications)

Use four paragraph marks:

Eli Whitney

Young Eli Whitney was always very good at mending everything in his father's workshop. Once when he was a boy, he even took apart one of his father's watches and put it back together again so well that no one ever knew it had been opened. In 1793 when Whitney was visiting a friend in the South, some cotton planters asked him if he would make a machine that could take the seeds out of cotton. Whitney agreed and invented the cotton gin. The principle of the cotton gin is really quite simple. It sifts the cotton through wires strung too close together for the seeds to pass through. A saw-tooth roller pulls the cotton along so that it passes through the wires.

The seeds all drop out, and then another roller with brushes takes the cotton off the saw teeth. Whitney's gin was worked by hand with a crank, but soon it was attached to a motor which turned the crank even faster. Before this invention, one person could clean the seeds out of 50 pounds of cotton in a day. Eli's machine, watched over by one person, cleaned 1000 pounds of cotton a day. Now the part of harvesting cotton that was the hardest and the most time-consuming, has been made simple by machine.

Adapted from *Who Invented It and What Makes It Work?* by Sarah Leslie (Platt & Munk)

STUDENT ACTIVITY 25B

Report on the Reports' Paragraphs
Check Your Work

DIRECTIONS: Compare your work to the writers'. Did you break the paragraphs in the same places?

The Foster Parent Plan

The cowbird is a "nest parasite." It lays its eggs in the nests of other birds. Cardinals are common victims of the cowbird in Florida, as are red-winged blackbirds and many other species. The cowbird is the only land bird in the United States with this trait.

Most of the birds chosen as foster parents will tolerate the extra egg and treat the hatchling as one of their own. However, cowbird eggs hatch quickly and the baby cowbird frequently out-grows and out-eats the offspring of the host birds. The cowbird chick is often the only survivor.

Not all birds will accept a cowbird egg laid in their nest. The birds of some species will remove the egg, some will abandon or rebuild the nest, and some will even build another nest layer right on top of the cowbird egg.

From *Florida's Fabulous Birds*
by Winston Williams (World Publications)

Eli Whitney

Young Eli Whitney was always very good at mending everything in his father's workshop. Once when he was a boy, he even took apart one of his father's watches and put it back together again so well that no one ever knew it had been opened.

In 1793 when Whitney was visiting a friend in the South, some cotton planters asked him if he would make a machine that could take the seeds out of cotton. Whitney agreed and invented the cotton gin.

The principle of the cotton gin is really quite simple. It sifts the cotton through wires strung too close together for the seeds to pass through. A saw-tooth roller pulls the cotton along so that it passes through the wires. The seeds all drop out, and then another roller with brushes takes the cotton off the saw teeth. Whitney's gin was worked by hand with a crank, but soon it was attached to a motor which turned the crank even faster.

Before this invention, one person could clean the seeds out of 50 pounds of cotton in a day. Eli's machine, watched over by one person, cleaned 1000 pounds of cotton a day. Now the part of harvesting cotton that was the hardest and the most time-consuming, has been made simple by machine.

Adapted from *Who Invented It and What Makes It Work?* by Sarah Leslie (Platt & Munk)

STUDENT ACTIVITY **26A**

What's the Main Idea?

DIRECTIONS: The following report by a fourth-grade student has four main ideas:

1 what a mosquito looks like

2 three important body parts

3 what mosquitoes eat and drink

4 the writer's personal response to her research

Using the paragraph mark (⌐), show where each new paragraph should begin and write down its main idea in the margin.

The Marvelous Mosquito

   Have you ever looked at a large drawing of a mosquito? Here is what a mosquito looks like. It has two antenna, six legs, and two large eyes. The eyes are made up of millions of tiny little eyes stuck together. A mosquito has a long proboscis that it uses to suck your blood, and a blood sac called the abdomen where the digested blood goes. Like some insects it also has thorax which is a part of the neck. Did you know that male mosquitoes eat nectar, which is a sugary liquid that it sucks from flowers? The female mosquitoes drink the blood of warm blooded mammals, meaning us humans and other animals. When the female mosquito sucks the blood of a mammal, the mosquito injects saliva. The saliva is what makes you itch. Mosquitoes are marvelous living creatures, but in some places in the world like Africa, Egypt, and South America, they also spread a disease called yellow fever that makes people sick and even die. We need to find ways to control mosquitoes and to cure the diseases they cause. Isn't it amazing that we learned so much about this tiny insect?

Paragraph Power ○ Scholastic Professional Books

STUDENT ACTIVITY **26B**

What's the Main Idea?

Check Your Work

DIRECTIONS: Compare your paragraph decisions to the writer's.

The Marvelous Mosquito

Have you ever looked at a large drawing of a mosquito? Here is what a mosquito looks like. It has two antenna, six legs, and two large eyes. The eyes are made up of millions of tiny little eyes stuck together. **Main Idea: What a mosquito looks like**

A mosquito has a long proboscis that it uses to suck your blood, and a blood sac called the abdomen where the digested blood goes. Like some insects it also has thorax which is a part of the neck. **Main Idea: Three important body parts**

Did you know that male mosquitoes eat nectar, which is a sugary liquid that it sucks from flowers? The female mosquitoes drink the blood of warm blooded mammals, meaning us humans and other animals. When the female mosquito sucks the blood of a mammal, the mosquito injects saliva. The saliva is what makes you itch. **Main Idea: What mosquitoes eat and drink.**

Mosquitoes are marvelous living creatures, but in some places in the world like Africa, Egypt, and South America, they also spread a disease called yellow fever that makes people sick and even die. We need to find ways to control mosquitoes and to cure the diseases they cause. Isn't it amazing that we learned so much about this tiny insect? **Main Idea: The writer's personal response to her research**

Indicate the most appropriate paragraph for each of the following details:

The mosquito is a flyer so it has two wings. **Paragraph #_____**

Spraying insecticides or poisons will kill mosquitoes. **Paragraph #_____**

In warm, wet climates mosquitoes can cause a disease called malaria. **Paragraph #_____**

Draining swamps will prevent mosquitoes from breeding. **Paragraph #_____**

What's the Main Idea?, Part 2

DIRECTIONS:

1 Read the book report all the way through to understand it.

2 Reread to identify its main ideas.

3 Insert a paragraph mark (⌐) to show where a new main idea and, therefore, paragraph begins.

4 Write the main idea of each paragraph on the lines that follow the report.

Character Sketch: Rudi   **Book: Banner in the Sky**

Rudi is short for his age of 16. His hair is light blond and he has a fair complexion. He is always very polite and courteous to his elders. Rudi, though he is small, is very strong. He is always willing to do something for someone and he tries to help people whenever possible. Rudi is selfless because he risked his life to save Saro when he fell from the ridge even though Saro had been mean to Rudi and made it clear to him that he did not like him. In doing so, Rudi gave up the glory and satisfaction of being the first man to reach the top of the Citadel. Rudi is also courageous because he took risks. When Captain Winter was trapped in the trench, Rudi put his life on the line to try to save him. Rudi took his own clothes and tied them together to pull Captain Winter out. Rudi could have been pulled into the trench as well, but he insisted on taking that chance.

Rudi is very much like Robin in *The Door in the Wall*. Both Rudi and Robin were selfless because they risked their lives to save or help someone else. Rudi saved Captain Winter and Saro. Robin overheard the robbers planning to steal Brother Luke's gold, and woke up John and Luke to warn them. Then, as the robbers were chasing them, he cleverly tripped them with his crutch. Rudi risked his life twice to save Saro and Winter, and Robin warned John and Luke and saved them from the robbers. They were both very brave and unselfish.

Name _____ Date_____

Main idea of paragraph 1: _____

_____

_____

Main idea of paragraph 2: _____

_____

_____

Main idea of paragraph 3: _____

_____

_____

Main idea of paragraph 4: _____

_____

_____

What's the Main Idea?, Part 2
Check Your Work

DIRECTIONS: Check your work. Compare your paragraph decisions to the writer's.

Character: Rudi   Book: Banner in the Sky

Rudi is short for his age of 16. His hair is light blond and he has a fair complexion. He is always very polite and courteous to his elders. Rudi, though he is small, is very strong. He is always willing to do something for someone and he tries to help people whenever possible.

Main Idea: What Rudi looks like and how he treats people

Rudi is very selfless because he risked his life to save Saro when he fell from the ridge even though Saro had been mean to Rudi and made it clear to him that he did not like him. In doing so, Rudi gave up the glory and satisfaction of being the first man to reach the top of the Citadel.

Main Idea: What Rudi did to show he thought of Saro before himself

Rudi is also courageous because he took risks. When Captain Winter was trapped in the trench, Rudi put his life on the line to try to save him. Rudi took his own clothes and tied them together to pull Captain Winter out. Rudi could have been pulled into the trench as well, but he insisted on taking that chance.

Main Idea: What Rudi did to show he is courageous

Rudi is very much like Robin in *The Door in the Wall*. They were both very brave and unselfish. Both Rudi and Robin risked their lives to save or help someone else. Rudi saved Captain Winter and Saro. Robin overheard the robbers planning to steal Brother Luke's gold, and instead of running away, he woke up John and Luke to warn them. Then, as the robbers were chasing them, he cleverly tripped them with his crutch. Rudi risked his life twice to save Saro and Winter, and Robin warned John and Luke and saved them from the robbers. They were both very brave and unselfish.

Main Idea: How Rudi compares to Robin in *The Door in the Wall*

ASSIGNMENT PLANNER

1 Choose your topics:

Check the topics or subjects that you could write about.

a big surprise _____	a sport you like _____	a scary experience _____
your hobby _____	a humorous incident _____	a celebration _____
an accident _____	a favorite TV show _____	a family pet _____
a special place _____	a book or movie _____	your closet _____
a party _____	a relative or friend _____	your idea: _____

2 Select the form of writing:

essay _____

letter _____ (friendly ___ complaint ___ opinion ___ request ___ business ___)

news article _____

a review _____

"how-to" directions _____

opinion/recommendation _____

your own idea: _____

3 Write the topic and form of each assignment below.   Date due:

_____   _____

_____   _____

_____   _____

_____   _____

SAMPLE OUTLINE FOR A MULTI-PARAGRAPH REPORT

TOPIC: Snails

PARAGRAPH 1: Many different kinds

- ☀ wheel snails
- ☀ limpets
- ☀ elodeas
- ☀ land snails

PARAGRAPH 2: Where to look for them

- ☀ near algae (which they eat)
- ☀ near pond leaves
- ☀ a piece of log in a pond

PARAGRAPH 3: Bodies of snails

- ☀ mouth on the underside of feet
- ☀ shells protect from enemies
- ☀ shells are brown or black

PARAGRAPH 4: Enemies

- ☀ fish, snake, water bird, leech

PARAGRAPH 5

Closing: Why pond snails are important

Paragraph Power ∘ Scholastic Professional Books

Name _____ Date_____

Report and Essay Editing Checklist

DIRECTIONS: Review your writing and check off what you've done.

Title of Report or Essay _____

1 The introductory paragraph introduces the main topic of my report
in an interesting way. . . . . ☐

2 Each body paragraph has its own main idea, with an opening sentence
that introduces the idea. . . . . ☐

3 Each body paragraph provides details that support its main idea. . . . . ☐

4 The closing sentence of each body paragraph makes a connection,
or transition, to the main idea of the paragraph that follows. . . . . ☐

5 The final paragraph sums up what I've learned about my topic.
My report ends with a closing sentence. . . . . ☐

6 My report is interesting to read. . . . . ☐

Plans for improving my paragraphs:

_____

_____

_____

_____

_____

_____

PRIME TIME TO TEACH

DIALOGUE
RULES

MINI-LESSON

Paragraphing Dialogue

INTRODUCTION: My students love to include dialogue in their stories, with varying degrees of success. The problem, of course, is that dialogue writing has its own special rules, such as starting a new paragraph each time there's a change in speakers—no matter how brief that paragraph may be. This lesson addresses important rules to get your students off to a good start.

MATERIALS

☀ Individual copies and overhead transparency of Student Activity 28 (page 111)

·············· SUGGESTIONS FOR TEACHING THE LESSON··············

1 Before class, copy the following passage on a chart, chalkboard, or overhead:

> **Temporary Forgetfulness, Part I**
>
> "Yeah, it's my birthday!" I squealed as I hopped out of bed and skipped down the hall. "Hi Mom," I said. "Can you guess what today is?"
>
> "Friday," muttered my mother. "Now get dressed!"
>
> I stood there shocked as my mother disappeared down the stairs. "Dad!" I yelled. "Ya know what today is?"
>
> "Not now, Harvey," my father said while putting on his tie. "I'm late for work."
>
> "Great!" I thought. "My parents forgot my birthday."

2 Ask students to read the passage to themselves and then call out what they notice about how the dialogue is structured. Write down their responses. Possibilities include:

☀ "Start a paragraph for a different speaker."

☀ "Indent the first line of a paragraph."

☀ "A paragraph can combine action and description with dialogue."

3 Distribute Activity 28, give students about 15 minutes to complete it, and have them share their responses as a class, using an overhead of the activity as a guide. Discuss why it's important to follow dialogue rules. Guide students toward understanding that they help readers to "see" conversations: Who is talking, what they're saying and feeling, and the circumstances surrounding the exchange.

Untangle the Dialogue

DIRECTIONS: Read the second half of the story "Temporary Forgetfulness" to see how it ends. Then reread it to find each sentence that should introduce a new paragraph. Place a paragraph mark (⌐) at the start of those sentences.

Temporary Forgetfulness, Part II

"Cut that out, creep," my brother Pat yelled from next door. "Quit slamming the door!" I bounced down on my bed, about to cry. Zoom! The door burst open and in came Melvin, my little brother, on his toy horse, Horsie. "Harvey?" said Melvin. "What?" I said crossly. "May I please borrow your scissors?" "Take 'em," I muttered. "Good!" squealed Melvin as he grabbed the scissors and sped away on his horse. I decided not to say anything until the next day, so if they forgot for the rest of the day I could snag them tomorrow. That would make them feel real guilty that they forgot my birthday. When I came home after school that day, I saw Melvin and Horsie speeding into my room. I marched up the stairs, fell down, and marched up again. I crashed through the doorway expecting to see Melvin ransacking my room. "Surprise!" In my room was the whole family, Mom, Dad, Melvin, and Pat. "Happy birthday, Harvey!" they cheered. So they didn't forget my birthday after all!

Untangle the Dialogue
Check Your Work

DIRECTIONS: Compare your work to the writer's. Did you break the dialogue in the same places?

Temporary Forgetfulness, Part II

"Cut that out, creep," my brother Pat yelled from next door. "Quit slamming the door!"

I bounced down on my bed, about to cry.

Zoom! The door burst open and in came Melvin, my little brother, on his toy horse, Horsie. "Harvey?" said Melvin.

"What?" I said crossly.

"May I please borrow your scissors?"

"Take 'em," I muttered.

"Good!" squealed Melvin as he grabbed the scissors and sped away on his horse.

I decided not to say anything until the next day, so if they forgot for the rest of the day I could snag them tomorrow. That would make them feel real guilty that they forgot my birthday.

When I came home after school that day, I saw Melvin and Horsie speeding into my room. I marched up the stairs, fell down, and marched up again. I crashed through the doorway expecting to see Melvin ransacking my room.

"Surprise!" In my room was the whole family, Mom, Dad, Melvin, and Pat. "Happy birthday, Harvey!" they cheered. So they didn't forget my birthday after all!

MINI-LESSON 18

Discovering Dialogue Rules in Literature

INTRODUCTION: There's no better place to find models of effective dialogue—and of how that dialogue is paragraphed—than in high-quality children's literature. This lesson, based on one of my favorite children's books, shows students how a professional writer treats dialogue.

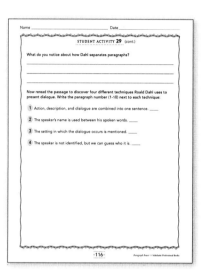

MATERIALS

☀ Individual copies of Student Activities 29 (page 115–116) and 30 (page 117)

☀ Lined paper and pencils for writing

·············· SUGGESTIONS FOR TEACHING THE LESSON ···············

1. Introduce the lesson. Say something like: "Roald Dahl, an author of humorous stories, is a skilled writer of dialogue. If any of you have read his book *Matilda*, you will never forget Miss Trunchbull. At the age of five and a half, Matilda entered a school run by Miss Trunchbull. Dahl describes Miss Trunchbull as 'a gigantic holy terror, a fierce tyrannical monster who frightened the life out of the pupils...' Miss Trunchbull terrified even Matilda's sweet, caring teacher, Miss Honey.

   "In one chapter, Miss Trunchbull is roaring mad because someone has put a stink bomb in her study. She is sure that Matilda, who had just started school that day, is guilty. Miss Honey, Matilda's good-natured teacher, is certain that Matilda is innocent. Let's look at the dialogue between Miss Trunchbull and Miss Honey."

2. Distribute the copies of Activity 29 and lined paper. Ask students to read the passage to themselves to get the gist of the story, and then reread it to "discover" rules for dialogue writing. Have them write the rules on the lined paper.

3 Discuss their discoveries as a class. Students may notice that Dahl uses "speaker tags" to tell readers that someone is talking. He begins a new paragraph whenever a different character starts speaking. He punctuates and formats dialogue in specific ways, such as indenting each paragraph, putting quotes around the speaker's exact words, and inserting end marks before the closing quotation marks.

4 Assemble a list of dialogue writing customs. It might look something like this:

Dialogue Writing Customs

1. Start a new paragraph when a different character starts speaking.

2. Use speaker tags to identify who's speaking (said, asked, wondered, shouted, etc.).

3. Punctuate the dialogue:

   ☀ Place quotation marks around speaker's words.

   ☀ Use commas.

   ☀ Put end marks (periods, question marks, and exclamation points) inside final quotation mark.

---

5 For extra practice, hand out Activity 30.

STUDENT ACTIVITY **29**

Who's Saying What?

DIRECTIONS: Read the humorous passage below from *Matilda* by Roald Dahl. The school's headmistress has accused Matilda of planting a "stink bomb" in her study. Matilda's teacher, Miss Honey, is trying to defend Matilda. Notice how Dahl helps us keep track of who is talking and who is listening.

"I must tell you, Headmistress, she said that you are completely mistaken about Matilda putting a stink-bomb under your desk."

"I am never mistaken, Miss Honey!"

"But Headmistress, the child only arrived in school this morning and came straight to the classroom..."

"Don't argue with me, for heaven's sake, woman! This little brute Matilda or whatever her name is has stink-bombed my study! There's no doubt about it! Thank you for suggesting it."

"But I didn't suggest it, Headmistress."

"Of course you did! Now what is it you want, Miss Honey? Why are you wasting my time?"

"I came to talk about Matilda, Headmistress. I have extraordinary things to report about the child. May I please tell you what happened in class just now?"

"I suppose she set fire to your skirt and scorched your knickers!"

"No, no!" Miss Honey cried out. "Matilda is a genius."

At the mention of this word, Miss Trunchbull's face turned purple and her whole body seemed to swell up like a bullfrog's. "A genius!" she shouted. "What piffle is this you are talking, Madam?" You must be out of your mind. I have her father's word that the child is a gangster!"

STUDENT ACTIVITY **29** (cont.)

What do you notice about how Dahl separates paragraphs?

_____

_____

_____

Now reread the passage to discover four different techniques Roald Dahl uses to present dialogue. Write the paragraph number (1-10) next to each technique:

1 Action, description, and dialogue are combined into one sentence. _____

2 The speaker's name is used between his spoken words. _____

3 The setting in which the dialogue occurs is mentioned. _____

4 The speaker is not identified, but we can guess who it is. _____

Speaking of Paragraphs

DIRECTIONS: The following story contains a lot of dialogue but no paragraph breaks. Place paragraph marks (⌐) wherever a new paragraph should begin.

My Fear

"Suzy, please come to the front desk," said the nurse through the intercom. I walked into the doctor's office trembling with fear. "Hello," my name is Dr. Smith. Have a seat." Cautiously I sat down on the chair. I wished my mother was right there with me. Dr. Smith pulled out something that looked like an over-grown needle. Before he even had a chance to speak, I screamed as loud as I could. After I finally calmed down, I asked almost in tears, "Do I have to go through with this?" "Kid, you already did." "What!" I yelled. "You see while you were screaming your head off, I quickly yanked your tooth out." Suddenly I felt a place in my upper jaw where a tooth was missing. "It's gone! It's gone! It's all over," I yelled. "You were really brave," said Dr. Smith. "Thank you," I said. I dreaded this day ever since I was a little child. But now I had made it through.

STUDENT ACTIVITY **30B**

Speaking of Paragraphs
Check Your Work

DIRECTIONS: Compare your work to the writer's. Did you break the dialogue in the same places? You should have ten paragraph marks.

My Fear

"Suzy, please come to the front desk," said the nurse through the intercom. I walked into the doctor's office trembling with fear.

"Hello," my name is Dr. Smith. Have a seat."

Cautiously I sat down on the chair. I wished my mother was right there with me. Dr. Smith pulled out something that looked like an overgrown needle. Before he even had a chance to speak, I screamed as loud as I could.

After I finally calmed down, I asked almost in tears, "Do I have to go through with this?"

"Kid, you already did."

"What!" I yelled.

"You see while you were screaming your head off, I quickly yanked your tooth out."

Suddenly I felt a place in my upper jaw where a tooth was missing. "It's gone! It's gone! It's all over," I yelled.

"You were really brave," said Dr. Smith.

"Thank you," I said. I dreaded this day ever since I was a little child. But now I had made it through.

Paragraph Power ∘ Scholastic Professional Books

FUN AND FAST DIALOGUE-WRITING ASSIGNMENTS

With these assignments, your students will be able to practice dialogue-writing skills, and have fun in the process.

IDEA 1: You are a student in a boarding school. On the hallway floor, someone has created a chalk drawing of the headmistress…with a mustache. Because you are known to be a good artist, the headmistress suspects you are the culprit and has ordered you and your teacher to meet with her in the office immediately. Use as many paragraphs as you need to write the dialogue and action at this meeting. Give your piece a suspenseful ending.

IDEA 2: You wake up happy because it is your birthday. You hop out of bed and run to the kitchen for breakfast with your family. Your conversation is about ordinary things—homework, chores, plans for the day. No one mentions your birthday. Use as many paragraphs as you need to write dialogue and action at this breakfast. Give your piece a happy ending.

IDEA 3: You've arrived at a dinner party to celebrate a family member's graduation from college. You learn that someone named "Aunt Delma" has prepared the dinner. You recognize her name from a story you read in *Horror Magazine*. Aunt Delma was the cook who poisoned a cake! Though hungry, you turn down each course she serves. Use as many paragraphs as you need to write dialogue and action at this dinner. Give your piece a humorous ending.

TIPS FOR WRITING DIALOGUE

☀ Use "speaker tags" to tell your reader that someone is talking (for example: said, asked, shouted, whispered, exclaimed, and replied).

☀ Begin a new paragraph whenever a different character starts speaking.

☀ Punctuate and format the dialogue:

   ○ Indent each paragraph.

   ○ Put quotation marks around the speaker's exact words.

   ○ Capitalize the first word the speaker says.

   ○ Insert additional punctuation (, . ! ?) before the closing quotation marks.

Paragraph Power ○ Scholastic Professional Books

Strategies for Building Students' Writing Skills All Year Long

☀ Set aside class time at least three days each week for your students to write for 40 to 60 minutes.

☀ Have your students develop a list of topics that they know and care about. Tell them to refer to this list when they need a writing idea.

☀ To help your students improve their first-draft writings, post a sign-up list for writing conferences with you. For more tips on conferring and revising, read *Teaching Writing: A Workshop Approach* (Scholastic).

☀ Plan mini-lessons that focus on the elements of good writing. See *25 Mini-Lessons for Teaching Writing* by Adele Fiderer and *Brighten Up Boring Beginnings and Other Quick Writing Lessons* by Laura Robb, both published by Scholastic, for student activity forms.

☀ Develop writing self-assessment checklists for your students to use throughout the year.

☀ Set aside time for your students to read aloud their writing to the class. Encourage their classmates to ask questions and offer suggestions for improving a draft.

☀ Photocopy examples of good writing onto an overhead transparency for a class discussion of what makes each one "good."

☀ Ask your students to share the word pictures and beautiful language that they find in the books they read. Using pieces of chart paper, keep a running list of notable passages.

☀ Have your students keep writers' notebooks—places where they can record ideas for writing as well as examples of good writing they find in literature. Ralph Fletcher's *Breathing In, Breathing Out* (Heinemann) and *Hey World, Here I Am* (HarperTrophy), Jean Little's fictional account of a girl who keeps a writer's notebook, will encourage notebook writing.

☀ Stock your classroom library with memoirs by authors of children's novels to help your students find the meaningful stories in their own lives.

RUBRIC FOR ASSESSING PARAGRAPHING SKILLS

Key Elements of an Excellent Writing Performance

_____ Organizes information logically in paragraphs

_____ Introduces the topic in the opening paragraph

_____ Includes a main idea for each paragraph, with an opening sentence that introduces that idea

_____ Develops each paragraph's main idea with accurate supporting details

_____ Writes a closing sentence for each paragraph that connects to the next paragraph's topic

_____ Concludes with a closing paragraph that sums up the topic and leaves the reader satisfied

_____ Demonstrates an excellent understanding of the writing topic

_____ Spells words and uses punctuation correctly

Scoring Guide

8 check marks: Proficient. All elements are evident to a high degree.

5–7 check marks: Capable. Some elements are developed well, others adequately.

2–4 check marks: Satisfactory. Some elements are adequately developed. Others are not.

0–1 check marks: Beginning. No key elements are adequately developed.

Paragraph Power ○ Scholastic Professional Books

RUBRIC FOR ASSESSING LETTER WRITING

Evaluative Criteria

_____ The first paragraph of a business letter states the writer's purpose for writing. The final paragraph ends with a closing statement.

_____ The body of a friendly letter or a business letter is appropriate for the writer's purpose. A friendly letter is conversational in tone. Anecdotes, descriptions, and details make it interesting to read. The body of a business letter has a clear message that relates to the writer's purpose.

_____ The format of the letter follows the planning form guidelines. The heading(s), salutation, and closing are correctly placed and provide the required information.

_____ The conventions of writing are followed (i.e., paragraphing, grammar, spelling, capitalization, and punctuation).

Scoring Levels

4 Proficient
All four criteria are evident to a high degree.

3 Capable
All four criteria are evident. A few errors in format, paragraphing, grammar, spelling, and/or punctuation may appear.

2 Satisfactory
The letter fulfills the writer's purpose. Some errors in format, paragraphing, grammar, spelling, and/or punctuation appear.

1 Beginning
The letter shows attempts to fulfill the writer's purpose, but ideas are not adequately developed. There are many errors in format, paragraphing, and/or the conventions of writing.

RUBRIC FOR ASSESSING RESEARCH-REPORT WRITING

KEY ELEMENTS	EVALUATIVE CRITERIA
_____ **Comprehension of Subject/Topic**	The writing indicates a complete understanding of the topic and reflects the use of a range of resources. The bibliography lists a variety of sources such as nonfiction texts, print and electronic articles, and audiovisual resources.
_____ **Writing Effectiveness**	
Idea Development	The writer develops relevant ideas clearly and fully. Information focuses on the topic. Details, examples, anecdotes, or personal experiences explain and clarify the information.
Organization	The writer organizes information logically in paragraphs. The introductory and closing paragraphs are effective.
Language Usage	The writer uses clear and descriptive language. Details, anecdotes, and examples explain and clarify information.
Mechanics	The writer makes few errors in basic language conventions.

Scoring Levels

Comprehension of Subject/Topic is evident to a:

3 high degree

2 satisfactory degree

1 limited degree

**Writing Effectiveness
All four key elements are evident to a:**

3 high degree

2 satisfactory degree

1 limited degree

0 No key elements are adequately demonstrated; equal to a blank paper.

Paragraph Power ○ Scholastic Professional Books

Name _____   Date _____

WRITING RUBRIC TO SHARE WITH KIDS

Title/Topic _____   **Score** _____

KEY ELEMENTS	EVALUATIVE CRITERIA
_____ **Idea Development**	The topic/task is fully developed with relevant information. Details, examples, descriptions, or anecdotes support and clarify ideas.
_____ **Organization**	The information is organized in paragraphs. It has an introductory paragraph that engages the reader and a satisfying closing.
_____ **Language Usage**	The writing has lively and descriptive language. Precise verbs and specific nouns explain and clarify the information. Sentences vary in types and length.
_____ **Mechanics and Conventions**	There are few errors in punctuation, capitalization, and paragraphing. Sentences are complete. There are few or no run-ons or fragments.

Scoring Levels

The key elements are evident:

to a high degree	4 points
to a satisfactory degree	3 points
to a limited degree	2 points
to no degree	1 point

Comments: _____

_____

_____

Closing Thought

Now that your students are well on their way to constructing effective paragraphs, encourage them to apply what they know in their essays, reports, letters, and stories. Provide opportunities for them to write on their own, read aloud their best paragraphs, and post their work on classroom walls. To help them get started, distribute the reproducible on the next page.

Paragraph Power ○ Scholastic Professional Books

Choose a Topic and Start Writing!

DIRECTIONS: Personal experiences are great sources for paragraph-writing ideas. When you write about what you know, your writing is at its best. This form gives you topic ideas for one, two, and multi-paragraph pieces. Check off the ones that interest you. Or choose your own topic.

A. Write a one-paragraph description of

☀ your favorite class or school activity   ____

☀ something you're good at   ____

☀ a favorite place   ____

☀ a pet   ____

☀ your own idea _____

B. Write a two-paragraph letter to

☀ a teacher, relative, or friend, expressing your appreciation   ____

☀ a store manager, complaining about something you bought   ____

☀ a long-distance friend or family member, with some news
  or an invitation to visit   ____

☀ your own idea _____

C. Write a multi-paragraph essay about

☀ your best or worst vacation   ____

☀ how to give a great party   ____

☀ a funny, sad, lucky, or unusual experience you had   ____

☀ a favorite hobby such as stamp collecting, art,
  music, or camping   ____

☀ your own idea _____

Bibliography of Children's Literature and Resources

Byars, Betsy. *The Midnight Fox.* New York: Story House, 1968.

Byars, Betsy. *The Pinballs.* New York: Harper & Row, 1987.

Cleary, Beverly. *Dear Mr. Henshaw.* New York: William Morrow and Company, 1983.

Dahl, Roald. *James and the Giant Peach.* New York: Alfred A. Knopf, 1961.

Dahl, Roald. *Matilda.* New York: Viking Press, 1988.

De Angeli, Marguerite. *The Door in the Wall.* New York: Doubleday, 1949.

Free Stuff for Kids. New York: Meadowbrook Press, 2001.

George, Jean Craighead. *Julie of the Wolves.* New York: Harper & Row, 1972.

Hahn, Mary Downing. *Daphne's Book.* Boston: Houghton Mifflin Company, 1983.

Hesse, Karen. *Out of the Dust.* New York: Scholastic, 1997.

Irion, Robert. "Catch a Falling Star." *Highlights for Children,* August 1999.

James, Elizabeth, and Barkin, Carol. *Sincerely Yours—How to Write Great Letters.* Boston: Houghton Mifflin Company, 1993.

Leedy, Loreen. *Messages in the Mailbox.* New York: Holiday House, 1994.

Leslie, Sarah. *Who Invented It and What Makes It Work?* New York: Platt & Munk, 1976.

Lessac, Frané. *My Little Island.* New York: HarperTrophy, 1987.

Little, Jean. *Hey World, Here I Am.* HarperTrophy, 1991.

Lowry, Lois. *Anastasia Ask Your Analyst.* Boston: Houghton Mifflin Company, 1984.

Lowry, Lois. *Anastasia Krupnik.* Boston: Houghton Mifflin Company, 1979.

Milne, Lorus J. *The Field Guide to North American Insects and Spiders.* New York: Knopf, 1980.

Otfinoski, Steve. *Putting It in Writing.* New York: Scholastic, 1994.

Paterson, Katherine. *Bridge to Terabithia.* New York: HarperCollins Publishers, 1977.

Paterson, Katherine. *The Great Gilly Hopkins.* New York: Crowell, 1978.

Rowling, J.K. *Harry Potter and the Chamber of Secrets.* New York: Scholastic, 1999.

Rowling, J.K. *Harry Potter and the Goblet of Fire.* New York: Scholastic, 2000.

Rowling, J.K. *Harry Potter and the Prisoner of Azkaban.* New York: Scholastic, 1999.

Rowling, J.K. *Harry Potter and the Sorcerer's Stone.* New York: Scholastic, 1997.

Stokes, Donald. *Guide to Observing Insect Lives.* Boston: Little, Brown, 1984.

Ullman, James Ramsey. *Banner in the Sky.* New York: Lippincott, 1954.

Williams, Winston. *Florida's Fabulous Birds.* New York: World Publications, 1994.

Paragraph Power ○ Scholastic Professional Books